FIX 'N' FREEZE
PRESSURE
COOKER
MEALS IN AN INSTANT

100 Best **MAKE-AHEAD DINNERS** for Busy Families

ELLA SANDERS

CASTLE POINT BOOKS
NEW YORK

FIX 'N' FREEZE PRESSURE COOKER MEALS IN AN INSTANT
Copyright © 2019 by St. Martin's Press.
All rights reserved. Printed in the United States of America.
For information, address St. Martin's Press, 120 Broadway, New York, NY 10271.

www.stmartins.com
www.castlepointbooks.com

The Castle Point Books trademark is owned by Castle Point Publications, LLC.
Castle Point books are published and distributed by St. Martin's Press.

ISBN 978-1-250-23473-5 (trade paperback)
ISBN 978-1-250-23472-8 (ebook)

Design by Joanna Williams
Production by Mary Velgos

Images used under license from Shutterstock.com

Our books may be purchased in bulk for promotional, educational, or business use.
Please contact your local bookseller or the Macmillan Corporate and
Premium Sales Department at 1-800-221-7945, extension 5442, or by email at
MacmillanSpecialMarkets@macmillan.com.

First Edition: October 2019

10 9 8 7 6 5 4 3 2 1

CONTENTS

SECRETS TO SUCCESS

WHAT'S FOR DINNER? Imagine coming home after a long day and not needing to worry about the dinner dilemma. With *Fix 'n' Freeze Pressure Cooker Meals in an Instant*, you'll always have a delicious answer waiting to go from freezer to pressure cooker to dinner table in just minutes!

Electric pressure cookers have revolutionized cooking in the last few years. It's now possible to whip up pot roasts, long-simmering stews, and even ribs on a weeknight. But even if you already turn to a pressure cooker to help speed dinner to the table, the Fix 'n' Freeze method takes convenience to the next level with dozens of simple, family-friendly recipes you prep in advance, freeze, and then pop into your multi-cooker when you're ready to eat. With Fix 'n' Freeze, you'll enjoy:

Home-cooked, healthier meals. *Fix 'n' Freeze Pressure Cooker Meals in an Instant* offers a variety of great dinner recipes that beat frozen pizza and takeout to the table and help you feel good about what you're serving your family.

Time saved for what you really want or need to do. You choose how many meals you want to make in advance—a week's or even a month's worth!—and dedicate a few hours or more on a weekend to preparing, bagging, and freezing the ingredients. It's fun, easy, and even something you can do together as a family, because most of the work involves simple chopping and measuring. On serving day, you add some liquid to your pot—usually in the form of flavor-building stock—place the frozen meal into the multi-cooker, and pressure-cook it until done. Given that you don't have to do anything to the pot while it's cooking, it's a godsend for multitaskers who need to help kids with homework, return emails, and catch up on household chores—all while making a hot meal.

Money saved and less food waste. Too often, in the dinner crunch, it's tempting to eat out or turn to takeout more often than you (and your budget) would like. If that sounds like your life, and you're looking for a new way to get a home-cooked meal on the table every night for your family, then the Fix 'n' Freeze method may be just what you're looking for.

In a time when we're becoming more conscious about food waste, this method wastes less food because you buy only what you need, prep it, and freeze it. It doesn't have time to languish and spoil in the fridge, only to be tossed away. You may also find that it saves you money because you're sticking to your shopping list!

With the Fix 'n' Freeze method, you've got this dinner thing in the bag. Literally.

THE FIX 'N' FREEZE METHOD

Ready to get started and be rewarded with a freezer full of ready-to-cook meals? It's so simple!

1. Select and shop. First, choose the recipes you want to make. Then, make a list, checking to see what you already have on hand and what you need to buy. Next, head to the store and shop. If you're preparing a week's worth of dinners, you can shop in the morning and do the prep work in the afternoon. If you're planning two or more weeks of dinners, you may want to shop the day before so you can start prepping the following morning.

Many of the recipes use the same cuts of meat—namely, boneless, skinless chicken thighs, chuck roast, and pork shoulder. There are several reasons for that. First, you can take advantage of larger, more economical packages, such as those you might find at a warehouse club or a family pack at your supermarket. Also, these cuts tend to be a little less expensive. Most importantly, though, these cuts are the best fit for pressure cooking. Lean cuts like chicken breast and pork tenderloin can dry out too easily, leading to disappointment.

Some recipes require you to add a few ingredients on cooking day, including perishable items that don't freeze or pressure-cook well (for example, dairy, some herbs, vegetables that are meant to stay crunchy). If you're preparing a week's worth of meals, you may want to pick up all of these serving-day items at once to have on hand. For two or more weeks, it's better to buy the items later to avoid spoilage.

2. Knock out the prep. Roll up your sleeves and clear the countertops! To speed the prep work, you can chop onions and other vegetables in a food processor, and no one will be the wiser if you use pre-minced garlic. (Hint: If you do, a teaspoon of minced garlic is about one clove, so a tablespoon would be about three cloves.) If you're very pressed for time, you can even buy precut veggies. If you're making several recipes that require you to precook ground beef or turkey, you can cook all of the meat at once, and then divide it up as needed for the recipes. To make the meats freezer and multi-cooker friendly, they're chopped into small pieces. That way, they'll cook evenly, and you won't be left with something that's overcooked on the outside and still frozen in the center.

Once you've prepped your ingredients, you'll place them in gallon-size freezer bags and then label and seal the bags. Then you'll put the bags in round containers so that they freeze into a round shape that can be put directly in the multi-cooker.

3. Take it from freezer to pressure cooker to table. On serving day, you'll need to add liquid in order for the multi-cooker to come up to pressure. Most models need about a cup of liquid, but check your manual to see what your machine's particular requirements are and increase the liquid if necessary. To build flavor, the recipes in this book generally call for stock. In a pinch, you can use water, but you may want to taste and adjust the seasonings at the end to compensate. On pages 7–9, you'll find tasty recipes for homemade stock, but it's perfectly fine to use canned stock or a concentrated chicken, beef, or vegetable base in water. If you use frozen homemade stock, just add it to the multi-cooker first, set it on Sauté, and once it has melted, add your food and proceed with the recipe.

A few hints: If you're having a hard time releasing the frozen food from the plastic bag, you can hold it under warm running water for a minute or two and it should slide right out. The multi-cooker will take longer to come up to pressure than you're used to, sometimes 20 minutes or longer, because the food thaws out before it's cooked.

TROUBLESHOOTING TIPS

Something not going quite as expected? Check out some of the most common issues that can pop up, along with simple solutions.

Too much liquid remains. Pressure cookers require a certain amount of liquid to come up to pressure. The amount varies by model, but it's generally between 1 and 2 cups. In addition, the cooking method itself forces foods to release a lot of their liquid, and unlike in stovetop cooking, not much of that liquid is lost through evaporation. This means that when you open the lid, there may be a lot more liquid in the pot than you were expecting. To reduce your sauce and concentrate its flavor, turn the pot to Sauté and simmer the liquid for a few minutes until it reaches the desired consistency. If your dish includes a meat that can be easily overcooked, remove it to a plate before you reduce the sauce. You can also mix together a tablespoon of cornstarch with enough water to dissolve, stir it into the pot, and simmer for a few minutes until the sauce has thickened.

WHAT YOU'LL NEED

Along with your multi-cooker and a clean inner pot, here are some of the key items you'll want to have on hand in your kitchen.

Gallon-size freezer bags. For most recipes, you'll put your prep ingredients in these bags.

Marker or labels. Don't forget to label your prep bags with the name of the dish. It may be helpful to add the page number of the recipe, so you can quickly and easily find the serving day directions.

Round (7-inch diameter) freezer-safe containers. Because you'll be putting the frozen ingredients in the multi-cooker, you'll need to make sure the items will fit. By placing your sealed prep bag inside a round container, you'll ensure the items freeze in the shape you need. If you freeze the items flat, you'll never get them in the pot! Once the food is frozen, you can remove it from the container.

Instant-read thermometer. It's very important to take readings in several different spots to make sure the food is thoroughly cooked and there are no cold spots.

Silicone baking mitt(s). Wear these when releasing the pressure valve to protect yourself from the steam. They're also useful when removing the inner pot.

A 6- or 7-inch springform pan or baking pan with removable bottom. You'll need this pan if you plan to make lasagna.

Aluminum foil. Some recipes call for a foil sling to carefully lower in and remove cookware from the multi-cooker. To create this tool, you will need a sheet of aluminum foil about 18 to 20 inches long. Fold the two long sides toward the center to make a long sling. Tuck in the ends before closing the lid.

The pot won't come up to pressure. Because the food is frozen, it can take 20 minutes or more to defrost and come to pressure. But if it doesn't come up to pressure, check to make sure that the steam release handle has been switched to "sealing" and that you've included enough liquid.

Something other than steam comes out of the steam release handle. Return the handle to the sealing position and allow the pressure to release naturally. It's possible that foam has built up inside the pot or that the pot is overfilled. Be sure to clean it thoroughly afterward to avoid any blockages. Certain foods, especially starchy or dehydrated items, require a natural release. Refer to your owner's manual for more information.

The silicone sealing ring smells. The silicone ring tends to absorb cooking odors. Remove and wash it after every use, and let it dry thoroughly. If you are particularly bothered by the smell, you can use a separate ring for sweet and savory dishes.

The pot starts counting down before it has come to pressure. There is most likely not enough liquid. Open the pot, stir, add a bit more liquid, and try again. Dried foods, such as rice, dried beans, and dried fruit, will absorb liquid, so make sure you include enough.

Food is still frozen. There are variations by pot and by manufacturer, so your meals could take a little more or less than the stated time. If you open the pot and find that part of the food is still frozen, use a wooden spoon to break up the frozen section and stir well. You can either return it to pressure for a few minutes, or if it is almost done, turn the pot to Sauté and simmer with the lid off until it is cooked through.

CHICKEN STOCK

Homemade chicken stock is surprisingly simple to make with the help of your pressure cooker. Don't skip the important step of refrigerating the stock before freezing it. The fat will rise to the surface, so you can just skim it off.

MAKES: 6 cups   **PREP TIME:** 10 minutes   **PRESSURE TIME:** 30 minutes   **RELEASE METHOD:** Natural

PREP INGREDIENTS

2   pounds chicken wings, split

1   onion, halved

2   carrots, cut into 2 or 3 pieces

2   ribs celery, cut into 2 or 3 pieces

2   sprigs thyme

2   sprigs parsley

1   bay leaf

½   teaspoon whole peppercorns

1   teaspoon vinegar

Salt to taste

PREP DIRECTIONS

Place all the ingredients in the multi-cooker inner pot. Add 6 cups water, being sure not to fill the pot more than two-thirds full. Cook on high pressure for 30 minutes, and then let the pressure release naturally.

When cool enough to handle, strain the stock into a storage container and refrigerate until cold. Skim any fat from the surface. Portion into ½-cup or 1-cup servings and freeze.

BEEF STOCK

Roasting the short ribs or soup bones helps make a richer, more deeply flavored beef stock. If you use soup bones, choose meaty ones. Keep an eye on the liquid level in the multi-cooker, and don't go over two-thirds full. If you need to, you can always use a little bit less water.

MAKES: 6 cups   **PREP TIME:** 10 minutes   **PRESSURE TIME:** 60 minutes   **RELEASE METHOD:** Natural

PREP INGREDIENTS

3   pounds bone-in beef short ribs or beef soup bones

2   tablespoons olive oil

    Salt and pepper to taste

1   onion, halved

2   carrots, cut into 2 or 3 pieces

2   ribs celery, cut into 2 or 3 pieces

2   sprigs thyme

½   bunch parsley

1   bay leaf

2   teaspoons whole peppercorns

1   teaspoon vinegar

PREP DIRECTIONS

Preheat the oven to 400°F.

Rub the ribs with the oil, season with salt and pepper, and place on a sheet pan. Transfer the sheet pan to the oven and roast for 30 minutes.

Place the roasted ribs and the remaining ingredients in the multi-cooker. Add 6 cups water, being sure not to fill the pot more than two-thirds full. Cook on high pressure for 60 minutes, and then let the pressure release naturally.

When cool enough to handle, strain the stock into a storage container and refrigerate until cold. Skim any fat from the surface. Portion into ½-cup or 1-cup servings and freeze.

VEGETABLE STOCK

Dried mushrooms and a splash of soy sauce help boost the savory, umami flavor in this simple vegetable stock. If you don't have or can't find parsnips, you can substitute a potato.

MAKES: 6 cups   **PREP TIME:** 10 minutes   **PRESSURE TIME:** 20 minutes   **RELEASE METHOD:** Natural

PREP INGREDIENTS

- 2 leeks, well cleaned and cut into a few pieces
- 2 carrots, cut into 2 or 3 pieces
- 2 ribs celery, cut into 2 or 3 pieces
- 2 parsnips, cut into a few pieces
- 2 dried shiitake or porcini mushrooms
- 2 sprigs thyme
- ½ bunch parsley
- 1 bay leaf
- 2 tablespoons olive oil
- 1 tablespoon soy sauce
- ½ teaspoon whole black peppercorns
- Salt to taste

PREP DIRECTIONS

Place all the ingredients in the multi-cooker inner pot. Add 6 cups water, being sure not to fill the pot more than two-thirds full. Cook on high pressure for 20 minutes, and then let the pressure release naturally.

When cool, strain, portion into ½-cup or 1-cup servings, and freeze.

SOUPS

CHICKEN, CORN, AND RICE SOUP

Enjoy quick and delicious comfort with this smart use of leftover chicken. In just 15 minutes, you can serve soup that tastes like it came from your grandmother's stovetop. It's a perfect bowl of soothing for days when you or a loved one is feeling under the weather. If you prefer, swap noodles for the rice; add them after pressure cooking and simmer until tender.

SERVES: 4   **PREP TIME:** 5 minutes   **PRESSURE TIME:** 5 minutes   **RELEASE METHOD:** Natural (10 minutes)

PREP INGREDIENTS

- 2 cups cooked chicken, cut into bite-size pieces
- 2 tablespoons olive oil
- ½ onion, finely chopped
- 1 carrot, peeled and finely chopped
- 1 rib celery, chopped
  Salt and pepper to taste
- 1 cup frozen corn

SERVING DAY INGREDIENTS

- 3 cups chicken stock
- ¼ cup long-grain white rice
  Chopped parsley, for garnish (optional)

PREP DIRECTIONS

Combine the prep ingredients in a 1-gallon resealable freezer bag. Squeeze out the air, seal, label, and place in a round container to freeze into shape.

SERVING DAY DIRECTIONS

Add the stock, rice, and contents of the package to the multi-cooker inner pot. Cook on high pressure for 5 minutes.

Let the pressure release naturally for 10 minutes, and then manually release any remaining pressure. Garnish with the parsley, if using.

CHICKEN TORTILLA SOUP

Good news: flavorful soup doesn't require all-day simmering. With a rich tomato- and cumin-spiked broth and tender chicken, every spoonful of Chicken Tortilla Soup is a reason to celebrate your pressure cooker. For extra pizzazz beyond the crushed tortilla chips, create a toppings bar that includes shredded Monterey Jack cheese, jalapeño slices (fresh or pickled), diced avocado, chopped cilantro, and sour cream.

SERVES: 4   **PREP TIME:** 10 minutes   **PRESSURE TIME:** 8 minutes   **RELEASE METHOD:** Natural (10 minutes)

PREP INGREDIENTS

- 1 pound boneless, skinless chicken thighs, cut into 1½-inch pieces
- 1 (15.5-ounce) can black beans, drained and rinsed
- 1 (16-ounce) jar salsa
- 2 tablespoons tomato paste
- 1 tablespoon olive oil
- ½ cup frozen corn
- 1 onion, chopped
- 3 cloves garlic, minced
- 2 teaspoons ground cumin
- 1 teaspoon paprika
- 1 teaspoon dried oregano
   Salt and pepper to taste

SERVING DAY INGREDIENTS

2½ cups chicken stock
   Tortilla chips

PREP DIRECTIONS

Combine the prep ingredients in a 1-gallon resealable freezer bag. Squeeze out the air, seal, label, and place in a round container to freeze into shape.

SERVING DAY DIRECTIONS

Add the stock and contents of the package to the multi-cooker inner pot. Cook on high pressure for 8 minutes.

Let the pressure release naturally for 10 minutes, and then manually release any remaining pressure. Serve with crushed tortilla chips and any of the toppings suggested above.

HEARTY HAM AND BEAN SOUP

Satisfying beans and flavorful ham come together with vegetables in this classic that provides a quick yet filling meal. The secret ingredient: white (versus black) pepper that adds floral, earthy notes for a perfect finishing touch. If white pepper isn't in your stock of spices, it's fine to substitute black pepper; just add white pepper to the list for your next shopping trip and try it another time.

SERVES: 4 to 6   **PREP TIME:** 15 minutes   **PRESSURE TIME:** 5 minutes   **RELEASE METHOD:** Natural (10 minutes)

PREP INGREDIENTS

1   large potato, peeled and cubed

2   (15.5-ounce) cans Great Northern or cannellini beans, drained and rinsed

½   pound ham steak, cubed

1   small onion, chopped

1   carrot, sliced into ½-inch rounds

1   rib celery, sliced

¼   teaspoon white pepper

½   teaspoon dried marjoram

1   cup chicken stock

SERVING DAY INGREDIENTS

2 cups chicken stock

PREP DIRECTIONS

Bring a large pot of salted water to a boil over high heat. Add the potato and blanch for 2 to 3 minutes. Drain and set aside in a single layer to cool. (A kitchen towel is useful for this task.)

Add the potatoes and the remaining prep ingredients to a 1-gallon resealable freezer bag. Squeeze out the air, seal, label, and place in a round container to freeze into shape.

SERVING DAY DIRECTIONS

Add the stock and the contents of the package to the multi-cooker inner pot. Cook on high pressure for 5 minutes.

Let the pressure release naturally for 10 minutes, and then manually release any remaining pressure.

CHILE CORN CHOWDER

Wake up your usual soup repertoire with this delicious, creamy chowder that features green chiles. They add an extra pop of flavor without too much heat for sensitive palates. For those who like to live on the spicy side, just add a pinch of cayenne to notch up the heat. Sliced green onions are a great garnish option.

SERVES: 4   **PREP TIME:** 10 minutes   **PRESSURE TIME:** 5 minutes   **RELEASE METHOD:** Natural (10 minutes)

PREP INGREDIENTS

- 1   (14.75-ounce) can cream-style corn
- 1   (12-ounce) package frozen corn
- 1   onion, chopped
- 1   carrot, finely chopped
- 1   (4.5-ounce) can green chiles
- 1   teaspoon garlic powder
-      Salt and pepper to taste

SERVING DAY INGREDIENTS

- 2   cups chicken or vegetable stock
- ¼   cup instant potato flakes
- 1   cup whole milk or half-and-half
- 2   tablespoons unsalted butter

PREP DIRECTIONS

Combine the prep ingredients in a 1-gallon resealable freezer bag. Squeeze out the air, seal, label, and place in a round container to freeze into shape.

SERVING DAY DIRECTIONS

Add the stock and the contents of the package to the multi-cooker inner pot. Cook on high pressure for 5 minutes.

Let the pressure release naturally for 10 minutes, and then manually release any remaining pressure. Stir in the potato flakes, milk, and butter.

BROCCOLI CHEDDAR SOUP

You can whip up this restaurant-quality soup in your own kitchen whenever you crave it. With the prep ingredients waiting in the freezer, the cheesy family favorite goes from pressure cooker to soup bowls in just 10 minutes. For a special treat, serve in sourdough bread bowls.

SERVES: 4　　**PREP TIME:** 10 minutes　　**PRESSURE TIME:** 5 minutes　　**RELEASE METHOD:** Natural (5 minutes)

PREP INGREDIENTS

- 1　pound broccoli, cut into bite-size pieces, stems peeled and thinly sliced
- ½　onion, minced or grated
- 1　carrot, shredded
- 2　cloves garlic, minced
- 1　cup chicken or vegetable stock
- 1　teaspoon mustard powder
- 　Salt and pepper to taste

SERVING DAY INGREDIENTS

- 1　cup chicken or vegetable stock
- 4　ounces (about 1 cup) shredded Cheddar cheese
- 2　tablespoons unsalted butter
- ½　cup heavy cream or half-and-half

PREP DIRECTIONS

Combine the prep ingredients in a 1-gallon resealable freezer bag. Squeeze out the air, seal, label, and place in a round container to freeze into shape.

SERVING DAY DIRECTIONS

Add the stock and the contents of the package to the multi-cooker inner pot. Cook on high pressure for 5 minutes.

Let the pressure release naturally for 5 minutes, and then manually release any remaining pressure.

Gradually stir in the Cheddar cheese, butter, and heavy cream until the cheese is melted. Using an immersion blender, puree the soup.

ROASTED TOMATO BASIL SOUP

A shortcut to incredible roasted flavor comes in a can. Using canned fire-roasted tomatoes gives you a jump start to making rich-tasting tomato soup. No one will know the difference when the ingredients blend perfectly in your multi-cooker. For a lighter soup, this recipe leaves out cream and butter, but you can stir in ¾ cup heavy cream and 2 tablespoons unsalted butter after releasing the pressure if you want a creamier result.

SERVES: 4   **PREP TIME:** 10 minutes   **PRESSURE TIME:** 5 minutes   **RELEASE METHOD:** Natural (10 minutes)

PREP INGREDIENTS

- 1   (28-ounce) can crushed fire-roasted tomatoes
- 1   small onion, chopped
- 3   cloves garlic, minced
- ½   cup packed fresh basil leaves
- 1   teaspoon sugar
  Salt and pepper to taste
  Pinch of crushed red pepper flakes (optional)

SERVING DAY INGREDIENTS

- 1½   cups chicken stock
- ¼   cup thinly sliced fresh basil
  Extra-virgin olive oil, for drizzling

PREP DIRECTIONS

Combine the prep ingredients in a 1-gallon resealable freezer bag. Squeeze out the air, seal, label, and place in a round container to freeze into shape.

SERVING DAY DIRECTIONS

Add the stock and the contents of the package to the multi-cooker inner pot. Cook on high pressure for 5 minutes.

Let the pressure release naturally for 10 minutes, and then manually release any remaining pressure. Stir in the basil, and drizzle with the olive oil.

KALE AND LENTIL SOUP

Full of flavor, this vegetarian soup is also packed with fiber and plant-based protein. It's a nourishing meal that tastes great and is great for you. Kale, onions, carrots, and olive oil are considered detoxifying foods that may help restore balance and energy when you're feeling mentally or physically rundown. But the best comfort may simply come from a bowl of delicious warmth.

SERVES: 4   **PREP TIME:** 15 minutes   **PRESSURE TIME:** 7 minutes   **RELEASE METHOD:** Natural (10 minutes)

PREP INGREDIENTS

- 1 cup dried brown lentils, picked over for debris and rinsed
- 3 cups chopped fresh kale (stems removed)
- 1 onion, chopped
- 1 carrot, chopped
- 1 rib celery, chopped
- ½ teaspoon dried thyme
- ½ teaspoon dried oregano
- 1 bay leaf
- 2 tablespoons tomato paste
- 2 tablespoons olive oil
- Salt and pepper to taste

SERVING DAY INGREDIENTS

- 2 cups vegetable stock
- ¼ cup chopped fresh parsley (optional)
- 2 teaspoons red wine vinegar
- Extra-virgin olive oil, for drizzling

PREP DIRECTIONS

Add the lentils to the multi-cooker along with enough water to cover by about 2 inches. Cook on high pressure for 10 minutes.

Let the pressure release naturally and drain the lentils, reserving 1 cup of the cooking water. (It's okay if the lentils are still a bit firm; they'll finish cooking in the soup.) Once the lentils are cool, add them, the reserved cooking water, and the remaining prep ingredients to a 1-gallon resealable freezer bag. Squeeze out the air, seal, label, and place in a round container to freeze into shape.

SERVING DAY DIRECTIONS

Add the stock and the contents of the package to the multi-cooker inner pot. Cook on high pressure for 7 minutes.

Let the pressure release naturally for 10 minutes, and then manually release any remaining pressure. Remove and discard the bay leaf. Stir in the parsley (if using) and the vinegar, and drizzle with extra-virgin olive oil.

ASIAN CHICKEN NOODLE SOUP

If you're in search of a chicken noodle soup that goes beyond the basic, this is your recipe. Shiitake mushrooms, fresh ginger, and lots of vegetables bring a depth of flavor that you'll love. Look for fresh udon noodles in the refrigerated case of your grocery store.

SERVES: 4 to 6   **PREP TIME:** 10 minutes   **PRESSURE TIME:** 7 minutes   **RELEASE METHOD:** Natural (5 minutes)

PREP INGREDIENTS

- 1 pound boneless, skinless chicken thighs, cut into 1½-inch pieces
- 1 carrot, sliced into rounds
- 3 or 4 dried shiitake mushrooms
- 1 jalapeño or serrano chile, thinly sliced (optional)
- 1 tablespoon chopped fresh ginger
- ¼ cup soy sauce
- 1 tablespoon brown sugar
- 1 tablespoon rice vinegar

SERVING DAY INGREDIENTS

- 3 cups chicken stock
- 8 ounces fresh udon noodles
- 1 teaspoon sesame oil
- 1 cup snow peas
- 1 cup torn bok choy leaves
     Bean sprouts, for garnish
     Sliced green onions, for garnish

PREP DIRECTIONS

Combine the prep ingredients in a 1-gallon resealable freezer bag. Squeeze out the air, seal, label, and place in a round container to freeze into shape.

SERVING DAY DIRECTIONS

Add the stock and the contents of the package to the multi-cooker inner pot. Cook on high pressure for 7 minutes.

Let the pressure release naturally for 5 minutes, and then manually release any remaining pressure.

Carefully remove the mushrooms and thinly slice them. Return them to the pot along with the udon noodles and sesame oil. Stir in the snow peas, add the bok choy, and garnish with the bean sprouts and green onion. Let stand for a few minutes until the noodles are heated through and the vegetables are slightly cooked but still crunchy.

MINESTRONE WITH PESTO

Satisfying minestrone can be ready so quickly when you prep the ingredients ahead and have them ready for pressure cooking straight from your freezer. If you wish, while the soup is cooking, cook 1 cup ditalini pasta on the stovetop and stir it into the soup when it's finished. Serve with a sprinkle of grated Parmesan cheese.

SERVES: 4 to 6   **PREP TIME:** 15 minutes   **PRESSURE TIME:** 5 minutes   **RELEASE METHOD:** Natural (10 minutes)

PREP INGREDIENTS

- 1   large Yukon gold potato, peeled and cubed
- 2   tablespoons olive oil
- 1   onion, chopped
- 1   carrot, sliced into rounds
- ¼   small head green cabbage, sliced
- 1   zucchini, chopped
- 1   cup frozen green beans
- 1   (15.5-ounce) can cannellini or Great Northern beans, drained
- ½   cup canned diced tomatoes
- 1   cup vegetable or chicken stock
- ¼   cup prepared pesto sauce
  Salt and pepper to taste

SERVING DAY INGREDIENTS

- 2   cups vegetable or chicken stock
  Grated Parmesan cheese, for garnish

PREP DIRECTIONS

Bring a large pot of salted water to a boil over high heat. Add the potatoes and blanch for 2 to 3 minutes. Drain and set aside in a single layer to cool. (A kitchen towel is useful for this task.)

Combine the cooled potatoes and the remaining prep ingredients in a 1-gallon resealable freezer bag. Squeeze out the air, seal, label, and place in a round container to freeze into shape.

SERVING DAY DIRECTIONS

Add the stock and the contents of the package to the multi-cooker inner pot. Cook on high pressure for 5 minutes.

Let the pressure release naturally for 10 minutes, and then release any remaining pressure. Garnish with the grated Parmesan cheese.

POTATO LEEK SOUP

This comfort-food classic can be on your table with only seven ingredients—most of which you probably already have on hand. One simple blanching step keeps the potatoes from becoming grainy in the freezer. For a richer version, stir in ½ cup heavy cream or half-and-half after the soup is done cooking.

SERVES: 4   **PREP TIME:** 15 minutes   **PRESSURE TIME:** 8 minutes   **RELEASE METHOD:** Natural

PREP INGREDIENTS

- 4 medium red or Yukon gold potatoes, peeled and cubed
- 3 large leeks, white part only, well cleaned and sliced
- 2 tablespoons unsalted butter
- 2 tablespoons chopped fresh parsley
- ¼ teaspoon ground thyme
- 1 cup chicken or vegetable stock
  Salt and pepper to taste

SERVING DAY INGREDIENTS

- 1½ cups chicken or vegetable stock

PREP DIRECTIONS

Bring a large pot of salted water to a boil over high heat. Add the potatoes and blanch for 2 to 3 minutes. Drain and set aside in a single layer to cool. (A kitchen towel is useful for this task.)

Combine the cooled potatoes with the remaining prep ingredients in a 1-gallon resealable freezer bag. Squeeze out the air, seal, label, and place in a round container to freeze into shape.

SERVING DAY DIRECTIONS

Add the stock and the contents of the package to the multi-cooker inner pot. Cook on high pressure for 8 minutes, and then let the pressure release naturally. If desired, use an immersion blender to puree the soup.

BUTTERNUT SQUASH SOUP

To serve up this sweet and creamy fall and winter favorite even faster, pick up precut butternut squash at the supermarket. You'll be enjoying every spoonful that much sooner. For a little crunch, garnish each bowl with a few pumpkin seeds.

SERVES: 4 to 6   **PREP TIME:** 10 minutes   **PRESSURE TIME:** 8 minutes   **RELEASE METHOD:** Natural

PREP INGREDIENTS

1   (3- to 4-pound) butternut squash, peeled, seeded, and cut into 1-inch cubes

1   onion, chopped

2   cloves garlic, minced

2   tablespoons chopped fresh sage

1   cup vegetable or chicken stock

      Salt and pepper to taste

SERVING DAY INGREDIENTS

2   cups vegetable or chicken stock

3   tablespoons unsalted butter

½   cup heavy cream (optional)

      Pumpkin seeds, for garnish

PREP DIRECTIONS

Combine the prep ingredients in a 1-gallon resealable freezer bag. Squeeze out the air, seal, label, and place in a round container to freeze into shape.

SERVING DAY DIRECTIONS

Add the stock and the contents of the package to the multi-cooker inner pot. Cook on high pressure for 8 minutes, and then let the pressure release naturally. Stir in the butter and heavy cream (if desired). Use an immersion blender to puree the soup. Garnish with the pumpkin seeds.

SPLIT PEA AND HAM SOUP

You can savor this soup any night of the week when you use a ham steak and take the prepped ingredients from freezer to pressure cooker! It's a delicious winter dinner with an amazing aroma that will fill your kitchen and warm your soul. Top with croutons or flaky biscuits for an extra-special touch.

SERVES: 4 to 6   **PREP TIME:** 10 minutes   **PRESSURE TIME:** 15 minutes   **RELEASE METHOD:** Natural

PREP INGREDIENTS

- 1   pound dried green split peas, picked over for debris and rinsed
- 1   onion, chopped
- 2   ribs celery, chopped
- 1   teaspoon ground thyme
- ½   pound ham steak, finely chopped
- Salt and pepper to taste

SERVING DAY INGREDIENTS

- 4   cups chicken or vegetable stock
- 4   strips bacon (optional)
- Sour cream, for garnish (optional)

PREP DIRECTIONS

Combine the prep ingredients in a 1-gallon resealable freezer bag. Squeeze out the air, seal, label, and place in a round container to freeze into shape.

SERVING DAY DIRECTIONS

Add the stock and the contents of the package to the multi-cooker inner pot. Cook on high pressure for 15 minutes, and then let the pressure release naturally. Meanwhile, if desired, cook the bacon in a skillet until crispy. Transfer to a paper towel–lined plate to drain. Crumble the bacon over the soup and serve with dollops of sour cream.

BEANS AND GREENS SOUP

Beans and greens is a classic Mediterranean culinary combination that can be prepared in many ways. In this soup, smoked turkey, onion, and garlic bring rich flavor to the nutrient-packed beans and greens. What a simple and satisfying way to get your veggies!

SERVES: 2   **PREP TIME:** 10 minutes   **PRESSURE TIME:** 5 minutes   **RELEASE METHOD:** Natural

PREP INGREDIENTS

1   smoked turkey wing, meat removed and torn into bite-size pieces

1   (15.5-ounce) can cannellini or small white beans, drained and rinsed

1   onion, chopped

2   cloves garlic, chopped

8   ounces frozen collard greens

1   bay leaf

    Salt and pepper to taste

SERVING DAY INGREDIENTS

2   cups chicken or vegetable stock

¼   cup chopped fresh parsley (optional)

PREP DIRECTIONS

Combine the prep ingredients in a 1-gallon resealable freezer bag. Squeeze out the air, seal, label, and place in a round container to freeze into shape.

SERVING DAY DIRECTIONS

Add the stock and the contents of the package to the multi-cooker inner pot. Cook on high pressure for 5 minutes, and then let the pressure release naturally. Remove the bay leaf. If desired, stir in the fresh parsley.

VEGETABLE BEEF SOUP

This old-fashioned soup favorite, in fact, never gets old, but it does get quicker to prepare when you turn to freezer prep and your pressure cooker. Don't worry: cutting all that time simmering on the stovetop won't undercut the delicious home-style taste at all—you'll savor those spoonfuls of tender beef, potatoes, and vegetables.

SERVES: 4   **PREP TIME:** 15 minutes   **PRESSURE TIME:** 10 minutes   **RELEASE METHOD:** Natural

PREP INGREDIENTS

1   large potato, cubed

½   pound beef stew meat, cut into ½-inch cubes

1   onion, chopped

2   carrots, sliced

2   ribs celery, sliced

1   (8-ounce) can tomato sauce

Salt and pepper to taste

1   cup frozen peas

1   cup frozen green beans

SERVING DAY INGREDIENTS

3   cups chicken or vegetable stock

PREP DIRECTIONS

Bring a medium pot of salted water to a boil over high heat. Add the potato and blanch for 2 to 3 minutes. Drain and set aside in a single layer to cool. (A kitchen towel is useful for this task.)

Combine the cooled potatoes with the beef, onion, carrots, celery, tomato sauce, and salt and pepper in a 1-gallon resealable freezer bag. Place the peas and green beans in a separate bag. Squeeze out the air, seal, label, and place each bag in a round container to freeze into shape.

SERVING DAY DIRECTIONS

Add the stock and the contents of the larger package to the multi-cooker inner pot. Cook on high pressure for 10 minutes, and then let the pressure release naturally.

Set the pot to Sauté. Add the peas and beans and cook for a few minutes until hot.

CREAMY PUMPKIN SOUP

This velvety-smooth soup is very versatile, colorful, and easy to make. Serve it as a company-pleasing first course for fall and winter entertaining, or enjoy it any time for a warming lunch. You can use another winter squash such as butternut squash if you don't have pumpkin on hand. Garnish with cooked, crumbled bacon when you have a little extra time to prepare.

SERVES: 4 to 6   **PREP TIME:** 10 minutes   **PRESSURE TIME:** 5 minutes   **RELEASE METHOD:** Natural (5 minutes)

PREP INGREDIENTS

- 2 pounds pumpkin, peeled, seeded, and cut into 1-inch cubes
- 1 onion, finely chopped
- 3 cloves garlic, minced
- 2 tablespoons chopped chives
- ½ teaspoon ground ginger
- Pinch of nutmeg
- Salt and pepper to taste

SERVING DAY INGREDIENTS

- 2 cups chicken or vegetable stock
- 1 cup heavy cream

PREP DIRECTIONS

Combine the prep ingredients in a 1-gallon resealable freezer bag. Squeeze out the air, seal, label, and place in a round container to freeze into shape.

SERVING DAY DIRECTIONS

Add the stock and the contents of the package to the multi-cooker inner pot. Cook on high pressure for 5 minutes.

Let the pressure release naturally for 5 minutes, and then manually release any remaining pressure. Use an immersion blender to puree the soup and then stir in the heavy cream.

ROOT VEGETABLE SOUP

Make the most of cold-weather veggie offerings by bringing them together in a delicious soup. It's easy to make substitutions with the root vegetables—for example, swap sweet potatoes for white potatoes. Just keep the overall veggie amount the same. For extra flavor and color, you can top with bacon, chives, and shredded cheese.

SERVES: 4   **PREP TIME:** 15 minutes   **PRESSURE TIME:** 5 minutes   **RELEASE METHOD:** Natural

PREP INGREDIENTS

- 1   large potato, peeled and cut into 2-inch cubes
- 1   small celery root, peeled and cut into 2-inch cubes
- 2   medium parsnips, peeled and diced
- 1   carrot, chopped
- 3   shallots, minced
- 1   rib celery, minced
- 3   cloves garlic, minced
- 3   tablespoons extra-virgin olive oil
- Salt and pepper to taste

SERVING DAY INGREDIENTS

- 2   cups vegetable or chicken stock

PREP DIRECTIONS

Bring a large pot of salted water to a boil over high heat. Add the potato, celery root, and parsnips, and blanch for 2 minutes. Drain and set aside in a single layer to cool. (A kitchen towel is useful for this task.)

Transfer the cooled vegetables to a 1-gallon resealable freezer bag along with the remaining prep ingredients. Squeeze out the air, seal, label, and place in a round container to freeze into shape.

SERVING DAY DIRECTIONS

Add the stock and the contents of the package to the multi-cooker inner pot. Cook on high pressure for 5 minutes.

Let the pressure release naturally. Use an immersion blender to puree the soup.

VEGETABLES

MISO-BROWN SUGAR CARROTS

A sweet and savory miso glaze brings out magic in carrots. It's worth keeping miso, a delicious soybean paste, on hand to add flavor to all kinds of soups, fish dishes, and vegetables. Make sure to look for white miso, not red, which has a stronger flavor that could overwhelm, in the refrigerated section of your grocery store.

SERVES: 4 to 6 **PREP TIME:** 5 minutes **PRESSURE TIME:** 4 minutes **RELEASE METHOD:** Manual

PREP INGREDIENTS

- 1½ pounds carrots, peeled and cut into 2-inch slices
- 2 tablespoons white miso
- 1 tablespoon packed brown sugar
- 1 tablespoon canola oil
- 1 tablespoon soy sauce

SERVING DAY INGREDIENTS

- 1 cup vegetable stock

PREP DIRECTIONS

Combine the prep ingredients in a 1-gallon resealable freezer bag. Squeeze out the air, seal, label, and place in a round container to freeze into shape.

SERVING DAY DIRECTIONS

Add the stock and the contents of the package to the multi-cooker inner pot. Cook on high pressure for 4 minutes. Manually release the pressure.

SOY-GINGER CARROTS

It's natural to want to put the focus and planning on your main dishes, but this vegetable might steal the dinner show when you serve it. And it takes such little effort for the tasty results, with the help of your freezer and pressure cooker! For more of a glaze, reduce the sauce at the end.

SERVES: 4 to 6   **PREP TIME:** 10 minutes   **PRESSURE TIME:** 4 minutes   **RELEASE METHOD:** Manual

PREP INGREDIENTS

- 1½ pounds carrots, peeled and cut into 2-inch pieces
- 1 tablespoon olive oil
- 1 tablespoon minced fresh ginger
- 1 tablespoon packed brown sugar
- 2 tablespoons soy sauce
- 1 teaspoon lime zest

SERVING DAY INGREDIENTS

- 1 cup vegetable stock

PREP DIRECTIONS

Combine the prep ingredients in a 1-gallon resealable freezer bag. Squeeze out the air, seal, label, and place in a round container to freeze into shape.

SERVING DAY DIRECTIONS

Add the stock and the contents of the package to the multi-cooker inner pot. Cook on high pressure for 4 minutes. Manually release the remaining pressure.

THAI PUMPKIN CURRY

Sweet pumpkin and coconut meet slightly salty and spicy red curry paste as amazing flavor complements. You can add some vegetarian protein by simply stirring in cubed tofu and letting it heat through for 5 minutes or so in the finished curry. Serve over jasmine rice.

SERVES: 4   **PREP TIME:** 10 minutes   **PRESSURE TIME:** 4 minutes   **RELEASE METHOD:** Manual

PREP INGREDIENTS

- 2 pounds pumpkin, peeled, seeded, and cut into bite-size pieces
- 1 green or red bell pepper, seeded and sliced
- 1 onion, thinly sliced
- 2 tablespoons packed brown sugar
- 2 tablespoons fish sauce
- 2 tablespoons red curry paste (or more to taste)

SERVING DAY INGREDIENTS

- ½ cup vegetable or chicken stock
- 1 cup coconut milk
- ½ cup thinly sliced basil leaves (Thai basil, if possible)

PREP DIRECTIONS

Combine the prep ingredients in a 1-gallon resealable freezer bag. Squeeze out the air, seal, label, and place in a round container to freeze into shape.

SERVING DAY DIRECTIONS

Add the stock, the coconut milk, and the contents of the package to the multi-cooker inner pot. Cook on high pressure for 4 minutes.

Manually release the remaining pressure. Stir in the basil leaves.

GREEK-STYLE BUTTER BEANS

Fasolia gigantes, or giant beans, is a traditional Greek dish that features giant lima beans simmered with tomatoes, garlic, and seasonings for hours. You can get a very similar flavor profile with butter beans cooked in your pressure cooker for just 15 minutes. They make a super side dish or even a filling vegetarian main dish when served with rice and a salad.

SERVES: 4 to 6   **PREP TIME:** 10 minutes   **PRESSURE TIME:** 5 minutes   **RELEASE METHOD:** Natural (10 minutes)

PREP INGREDIENTS

- 2   (15.5-ounce) cans butter beans, drained and rinsed
- ½   onion, chopped
- 2   plum tomatoes, grated or diced
- 4   cloves garlic, minced
- ¼   cup chopped fresh parsley
- ¼   cup olive oil
- 1   tablespoon honey
   Salt and pepper to taste

SERVING DAY INGREDIENTS

- 1   cup vegetable stock
- ¼   cup sliced almonds (optional)
- ¼   cup chopped fresh parsley (optional)
   Lemon wedges, for garnish

PREP DIRECTIONS

Combine the prep ingredients in a 1-gallon resealable freezer bag. Squeeze out the air, seal, label, and place in a round container to freeze into shape.

SERVING DAY DIRECTIONS

Add the stock and the contents of the package to the multi-cooker inner pot. Cook on high pressure for 5 minutes.

Let the pressure release naturally for 10 minutes, and then manually release any remaining pressure. Stir in the almonds and parsley, if using, and serve with lemon wedges.

NEW ORLEANS-STYLE RED BEANS

This Cajun classic pairs perfectly with white rice for a complete meal you can speed to the table and feel good about serving. If you want a meatier option, add up to 8 ounces sliced andouille sausage to the prep ingredients, or serve it on the side on the day you prepare the dish.

SERVES: 4   **PREP TIME:** 10 minutes   **PRESSURE TIME:** 5 minutes   **RELEASE METHOD:** Natural (10 minutes)

PREP INGREDIENTS

- 2 (15.5-ounce) cans small red beans, drained and rinsed
- 1 green bell pepper, seeded and chopped
- 1 onion, chopped
- 1 rib celery, chopped
- 4 cloves garlic, minced
- 2 tablespoons olive oil
- 1 tablespoon hot sauce
- 1 teaspoon Cajun seasoning
    Salt and pepper to taste

SERVING DAY INGREDIENTS

- 1 cup vegetable stock
    Thinly sliced green onion, for garnish

PREP DIRECTIONS

Combine the prep ingredients in a 1-gallon resealable freezer bag. Squeeze out the air, seal, label, and place in a round container to freeze into shape.

SERVING DAY DIRECTIONS

Add the stock and the contents of the package to the multi-cooker inner pot. Cook on high pressure for 5 minutes.

Let the pressure release naturally for 10 minutes, and then manually release any remaining pressure. Garnish with green onion.

CHICKPEAS WITH ARTICHOKES AND SUN-DRIED TOMATOES

Bring the rich flavors of the Mediterranean—oregano, rosemary, artichokes, olives, and sun-dried tomatoes—to any dinner, even on a busy weeknight! In 20 minutes, you can have this dish ready to serve with rice, orzo, or couscous for a taste adventure.

SERVES: 4   **PREP TIME:** 10 minutes   **PRESSURE TIME:** 5 minutes   **RELEASE METHOD:** Natural (10 minutes)

PREP INGREDIENTS

- 2 (15.5-ounce) cans chickpeas, drained and rinsed
- 1 onion, chopped
- 1 plum tomato, chopped
- 3 cloves garlic, minced
- ¼ cup chopped sun-dried tomatoes in oil
- 1 teaspoon dried oregano
- ½ teaspoon dried rosemary
- 2 tablespoons olive oil
- Salt and pepper to taste

SERVING DAY INGREDIENTS

- 1 cup vegetable stock
- ½ (9-ounce) package frozen artichokes
- ½ cup sliced black olives (optional)
- ¼ cup chopped fresh parsley (optional)

PREP DIRECTIONS

Combine the prep ingredients in a 1-gallon resealable freezer bag. Squeeze out the air, seal, label, and place in a round container to freeze into shape.

SERVING DAY DIRECTIONS

Add the stock and the contents of the package to the multi-cooker inner pot. Cook on high pressure for 5 minutes.

Let the pressure release naturally for 10 minutes, and then manually release any remaining pressure.

Set the pot to Sauté. Stir in the frozen artichokes and cook, stirring occasionally, until heated through. If desired, stir in the black olives and chopped fresh parsley.

CURRIED CHICKPEAS

Inspired by a traditional chana masala, this Indian dish is simple to prepare, wonderfully aromatic, and sure to become a favorite in your dinner rotation. For maximum flavor, toast the spices in a dry pan just until fragrant, and then let them cool before adding them to your freezer bag.

SERVES: 4   **PREP TIME:** 10 minutes   **PRESSURE TIME:** 5 minutes   **RELEASE METHOD:** Natural (10 minutes)

PREP INGREDIENTS

- 2 (15.5-ounce) cans chickpeas, drained and rinsed
- 3 cloves garlic, chopped
- 1 tablespoon minced ginger
- 1 jalapeño or serrano chile, seeded and minced (optional)
- 1 tablespoon ground coriander
- 1 tablespoon ground cumin
- 1 teaspoon ground turmeric
- 2 tablespoons tomato paste
- 1 cup canned diced tomatoes
  Salt and pepper to taste

SERVING DAY INGREDIENTS

- 1 cup vegetable stock
  Juice of ½ lime or lemon
- ¼ cup chopped cilantro

PREP DIRECTIONS

Combine the prep ingredients in a 1-gallon resealable freezer bag. Squeeze out the air, seal, label, and place in a round container to freeze into shape.

SERVING DAY DIRECTIONS

Add the stock and the contents of the package to the multi-cooker inner pot. Cook on high pressure for 5 minutes.

Let the pressure release naturally for 10 minutes, and then manually release any remaining pressure. Stir in the lime juice and chopped cilantro.

STEWS & CHILIS

MEXICAN BEAN STEW

This south-of-the-border stew is packed with nutritious ingredients that come together quickly and deliciously in your pressure cooker. The stew tastes great on its own or served over rice. To add even more bright flavor, top it with avocado, fresh cilantro, and a squeeze of lime juice.

SERVES: 4   **PREP TIME:** 10 minutes   **PRESSURE TIME:** 5 minutes   **RELEASE METHOD:** Natural

PREP INGREDIENTS

- 1   (28-ounce) can crushed fire-roasted tomatoes
- 1   (6.7-ounce) jar roasted red peppers, drained and sliced
- 1   (15.5-ounce) can dark kidney beans, drained and rinsed
- 3   tablespoons olive oil
- 1   cup frozen corn
- 1   jalapeño, chopped (seeded for less heat, if desired)
- 3   cloves garlic, minced
- 1   teaspoon ground cumin
- 1   teaspoon dried oregano
     Salt and pepper to taste

SERVING DAY INGREDIENTS

- 2   cups vegetable stock

PREP DIRECTIONS

Combine the prep ingredients in a 1-gallon resealable freezer bag. Squeeze out the air, seal, label, and place in a round container to freeze into shape.

SERVING DAY DIRECTIONS

Add the stock and the contents of the package to the multi-cooker inner pot. Cook on high pressure for 5 minutes. Let the pressure release naturally.

CHICKEN, CHORIZO, AND CHICKPEA STEW

A chicken dinner can be so much more than just a few variations on chicken breasts! This Spanish-style stew uses chicken thighs to give you top taste and tenderness for cheaper than chicken breasts. Chorizo and chickpeas combine with the chicken for an amazing medley of flavor. Serve with rice or couscous.

SERVES: 4 to 6   **PREP TIME:** 15 minutes   **PRESSURE TIME:** 10 minutes   **RELEASE METHOD:** Natural (10 minutes)

PREP INGREDIENTS

- 1½ pounds boneless, skinless chicken thighs, sliced into ½-inch strips
- ½ pound dried Spanish chorizo, thinly sliced
- 1 (15.5-ounce) can chickpeas, drained and rinsed
- 1 onion, chopped
- 3 cloves garlic, minced
- 2 teaspoons paprika
- 1 teaspoon dried oregano
  Salt and pepper to taste

SERVING DAY INGREDIENTS

- 1 cup chicken stock
  Chopped fresh parsley, for garnish (optional)

PREP DIRECTIONS

Combine the prep ingredients in a 1-gallon resealable freezer bag. Squeeze out the air, seal, label, and place in a round container to freeze into shape.

SERVING DAY DIRECTIONS

Add the stock and the contents of the package to the multi-cooker inner pot. Cook on high pressure for 10 minutes.

Let the pressure release naturally for 10 minutes, and then manually release any remaining pressure. If desired, garnish with chopped parsley.

BEEF AND GUINNESS STEW

It's easy to impress guests with tender beef, vegetables, and potatoes swimming in a rich, hearty sauce. This world-class stew is usually simmered for hours on the stovetop, chaining you to the kitchen and pulling you away from spending time with family and friends. But your multi-cooker makes flavor miracles happen in so much less time! Serve with Irish soda bread.

SERVES: 6 to 8   **PREP TIME:** 15 minutes   **PRESSURE TIME:** 20 minutes   **RELEASE METHOD:** Natural

PREP INGREDIENTS

2   pounds chuck roast, cut into 1-inch chunks

1   onion, chopped

2   carrots, peeled and cut into 2-inch pieces

1   rib celery, chopped

1   tablespoon Worcestershire sauce

2   tablespoons dehydrated onion flakes (optional)

2   tablespoons tomato paste

1   beef bouillon cube

1   sprig fresh rosemary or ¼ teaspoon dried rosemary

3   or 4 sprigs fresh thyme or ½ teaspoon dried thyme

   Salt and pepper to taste

SERVING DAY INGREDIENTS

1   cup Guinness

1   pound potatoes, peeled and cubed

2   tablespoons unsalted butter, softened

2   tablespoons all-purpose flour

   Chopped fresh parsley, for garnish

PREP DIRECTIONS

Combine the prep ingredients in a 1-gallon resealable freezer bag. Squeeze out the air, seal, label, and place in a round container to freeze into shape.

SERVING DAY DIRECTIONS

Add the Guinness and the contents of the package to the multi-cooker inner pot. Cook on high pressure for 20 minutes, and then let the pressure release naturally.

Meanwhile, place the potatoes in a large pot of salted water. Bring to a boil, lower the heat, and simmer until just tender. Drain. Stir the potatoes into the stew.

To thicken the stew, in a small bowl, mash together the butter and flour. Set the pot to Sauté and stir in the butter mixture until the sauce is thickened to the desired consistency. If you used fresh rosemary and thyme sprigs, remove and discard. Sprinkle your stew with chopped fresh parsley before serving.

ITALIAN SAUSAGE AND LENTIL STEW

Traditionally, this Tuscan-style recipe uses links of sausage, but to make it freezer friendly, all you need to do is simply take the sausage out of its casing and brown it in advance. Serve the savory stew with polenta, bread, or just as it is.

SERVES: 4 to 6   **PREP TIME:** 10 minutes   **PRESSURE TIME:** 5 minutes   **RELEASE METHOD:** Natural (5 minutes)

PREP INGREDIENTS

- 1   cup dried brown lentils, picked over for debris and rinsed
- 1   pound bulk mild Italian sausage, casings removed, browned, drained, and cooled
- 1   onion, chopped
- 3   cloves garlic, minced
- ¼   cup dry red wine
       Salt and pepper to taste

SERVING DAY INGREDIENTS

- 1   cup chicken stock

PREP DIRECTIONS

Add the lentils to the multi-cooker along with enough water to cover by about an inch. Cook on high pressure for 10 minutes.

Let the pressure release naturally and drain the lentils. Once cooled, add them to a 1-gallon resealable plastic bag along with the remaining prep ingredients. Squeeze out the air, seal, label, and place in a round container to freeze into shape.

SERVING DAY DIRECTIONS

Add the stock and the contents of the package to the multi-cooker inner pot. Cook on high pressure for 5 minutes.

Let the pressure release naturally for 5 minutes, and then manually release any remaining pressure.

CHICKEN AND SAUSAGE STEW

With garlic, balsamic vinegar, and dry red wine, comfort food meets sophistication in your pressure cooker. The full-bodied flavor doesn't call for full-time work in the kitchen, though. In less than 20 minutes, you can enjoy this stew served over polenta or with pasta.

SERVES: 4   **PREP TIME:** 15 minutes   **PRESSURE TIME:** 8 minutes   **RELEASE METHOD:** Natural (10 minutes)

PREP INGREDIENTS

- 1 pound boneless, skinless chicken thighs, cut into 1-inch pieces
- 1 pound Italian sausage, cut into 1-inch slices
- 2 bell peppers, seeded and sliced
- 1 onion, chopped
- 3 cloves garlic, minced
- 2 tablespoons balsamic vinegar
- ¼ cup dry red wine
- Salt to taste

SERVING DAY INGREDIENTS

- 1 cup chicken stock
- Sliced basil leaves, for garnish (optional)

PREP DIRECTIONS

Combine the prep ingredients in a 1-gallon resealable freezer bag. Squeeze out the air, seal, label, and place in a round container to freeze into shape.

SERVING DAY DIRECTIONS

Add the stock and the contents of the package to the multi-cooker inner pot. Cook on high pressure for 8 minutes.

Let the pressure release naturally for 10 minutes, and then manually release any remaining pressure. Garnish with sliced basil, if desired.

FRENCH-STYLE PORK WITH WHITE BEANS

The flavors of Provence shine through in this one-pot wonder. While white beans such as flageolet may be more authentic, cannellini beans are much easier to find and won't compromise the taste a bit. Just wait (not long!) until you scoop up the tender pork and beans.

SERVES: 4 to 6   **PREP TIME:** 15 minutes   **PRESSURE TIME:** 15 minutes   **RELEASE METHOD:** Natural

PREP INGREDIENTS

- 1½ pounds boneless pork shoulder, cut into 1-inch pieces
- 1 onion, chopped
- 1 rib celery, chopped
- 2 carrots, peeled and chopped
- 5 cloves garlic, minced
- 2 teaspoons herbes de Provence
- 1 bay leaf
- Salt and pepper to taste

SERVING DAY INGREDIENTS

- ½ cup dry white wine
- ½ cup chicken stock
- 1 (15.5-ounce) can cannellini beans, drained and rinsed
- Chopped fresh parsley, for garnish (optional)

PREP DIRECTIONS

Combine the prep ingredients in a 1-gallon resealable freezer bag. Squeeze out the air, seal, label, and place in a round container to freeze into shape.

SERVING DAY DIRECTIONS

Add the wine, the stock, and the contents of the package to the multi-cooker inner pot. Cook on high pressure for 15 minutes.

Let the pressure release naturally. The pork should be fork-tender and shred easily. Set the pot to Sauté. Stir in the beans and cook until heated through. If desired, garnish with chopped parsley.

PORK AND HOMINY STEW

Pozole, sometimes called *posole*, is a simple Mexican stew made with pork, hominy, and seasonings. The satisfying dish becomes even simpler and quicker to make in your pressure cooker. You can usually find canned hominy near the canned beans or near other Latin American products in the supermarket. Chopped fresh onion or shredded green cabbage makes a great (optional) garnish. Serve with warm corn tortillas to soak up the broth.

SERVES: 4 to 6   **PREP TIME:** 15 minutes   **PRESSURE TIME:** 15 minutes   **RELEASE METHOD:** Natural

PREP INGREDIENTS

- 1 pound pork shoulder, cut into 1-inch pieces
- 1 onion, chopped
- 3 cloves garlic, chopped
- 1 jalapeño, chopped (seeded for less heat, if desired)
- 1 (15-ounce) can red enchilada sauce
- 1 (4.5-ounce) can green chiles
- 1 teaspoon paprika
   Salt to taste

SERVING DAY INGREDIENTS

- 2 cups chicken or beef stock
- 1 (28-ounce) can hominy, drained and rinsed
- ¼ cup chopped fresh cilantro

PREP DIRECTIONS

Combine the prep ingredients in a 1-gallon resealable freezer bag. Squeeze out the air, seal, label, and place in a round container to freeze into shape.

SERVING DAY DIRECTIONS

Add the stock and the contents of the package to the multi-cooker inner pot. Cook on high pressure for 15 minutes.

Let the pressure release naturally. The pork should be fork-tender and shred easily. Using a slotted spoon, remove the pork to a bowl and shred with two forks.

Set the pot to Sauté and stir in the hominy. Return the pork to the pot. Cook until the hominy is heated through and the flavors have melded, about 5 minutes. Stir in the cilantro.

CAJUN TURKEY AND BLACK-EYED PEAS

Spice up any weeknight with this Southern chili-type dish! If you don't keep Cajun seasoning in your spice selection, it's a worthy addition. The mix of paprika, cayenne, garlic powder, and other herbs and spices is usually available in the spice aisle and gives a flavor kick to all kinds of foods, including fish, soups, stews, potatoes, and meats.

SERVES: 4 to 6   **PREP TIME:** 15 minutes   **PRESSURE TIME:** 8 minutes   **RELEASE METHOD:** Natural (10 minutes)

PREP INGREDIENTS

- 1 pound ground turkey, browned, drained, and cooled
- 2 (15.5-ounce) cans black-eyed peas, drained and rinsed
- 4 cloves garlic, minced
- 1 tablespoon Cajun seasoning
- 1 jalapeño pepper, thinly sliced (seeded for less heat, if desired)
- 2 tablespoons tomato paste
  Salt to taste

SERVING DAY INGREDIENTS

- 1 cup chicken stock

PREP DIRECTIONS

Combine the prep ingredients in a 1-gallon resealable freezer bag. Squeeze out the air, seal, label, and place in a round container to freeze into shape.

SERVING DAY DIRECTIONS

Add the stock and the contents of the package to the multi-cooker inner pot. Cook on high pressure for 8 minutes.

Let the pressure release naturally for 10 minutes, and then manually release any remaining pressure.

BLACK-EYED PEAS WITH SAUSAGE AND BUTTERNUT SQUASH

Enjoying black-eyed peas on New Year's Day is a Southern tradition meant to bring good luck. But after one taste of the combination of sweet butternut squash, smoked kielbasa, and hearty black-eyes, you won't want to save this stew for just one day of the year!

SERVES: 4   **PREP TIME:** 15 minutes   **PRESSURE TIME:** 7 minutes   **RELEASE METHOD:** Natural (10 minutes)

PREP INGREDIENTS

- 1   (15.5-ounce) can black-eyed peas, drained and rinsed
- 1   pound kielbasa sausage, sliced
- 3   cups cubed butternut squash
- 1   onion, chopped
- 1   rib celery, chopped
- 1   teaspoon paprika
- 2   bay leaves
- 2   tablespoons tomato paste
-     Salt and pepper to taste

SERVING DAY INGREDIENTS

- 1   cup chicken or beef stock

PREP DIRECTIONS

Combine the prep ingredients in a 1-gallon resealable freezer bag. Squeeze out the air, seal, label, and place in a round container to freeze into shape.

SERVING DAY DIRECTIONS

Add the stock and the contents of the package to the multi-cooker inner pot. Cook on high pressure for 7 minutes.

Let the pressure release naturally for 10 minutes, and then manually release any remaining pressure.

SPICY SAUSAGE AND CHICKPEA STEW

With satisfying vegetables, chickpeas, and seasoned sausage, this hearty stew is a complete meal. If your household's tastes tend toward the mild side, substitute sweet for hot Italian sausage. Sprinkle on a bit of grated Parmesan to serve, and pair with a crusty bread.

SERVES: 4 **PREP TIME:** 15 minutes **PRESSURE TIME:** 7 minutes **RELEASE METHOD:** Natural

PREP INGREDIENTS

- ½ pound hot Italian sausage, casings removed, browned, drained, and cooled to room temperature
- 1 onion, chopped
- 1 carrot, chopped
- 1 red bell pepper, seeded and chopped
- 1 rib celery, chopped
- 1 tablespoon minced garlic
- 1 cup canned diced tomatoes, drained
- 1 (15.5-ounce) can chickpeas, drained and rinsed

   Salt and pepper to taste

SERVING DAY INGREDIENTS

- 2 cups chicken or beef stock

PREP DIRECTIONS

Combine the prep ingredients in a 1-gallon resealable freezer bag. Squeeze out the air, seal, label, and place in a round container to freeze into shape.

SERVING DAY DIRECTIONS

Add the stock and the contents of the package to the multi-cooker inner pot. Cook on high pressure for 7 minutes, and then let the pressure release naturally.

BEEF AND BEAN CHILI

Every kitchen needs a classic chili recipe. You'll love this simple version that cooks up deliciously in an unbelievable 7 minutes! Chipotle peppers add a deep, smoky flavor that make it taste like the chili simmered for hours. Serve with your favorite chili toppings, such as shredded cheese, sour cream, crushed corn chips, diced avocado, chopped onion, and cilantro.

SERVES: 4   **PREP TIME:** 15 minutes   **PRESSURE TIME:** 7 minutes   **RELEASE METHOD:** Natural (5 minutes)

PREP INGREDIENTS

- 1 pound ground beef, browned, drained, and cooled
- 1 (15.5-ounce) can kidney or pinto beans, drained and rinsed
- 1 (14.5-ounce) can diced tomatoes, drained
- 1 bell pepper, seeded and thinly sliced
- 1 onion, chopped
- 2 cloves garlic, minced
- 2 tablespoons chili powder
- 1 teaspoon ground cumin
- 1 teaspoon dried oregano
- 2 teaspoons chopped canned chipotle pepper in adobo
- Salt to taste

SERVING DAY INGREDIENTS

- 1 cup chicken or beef stock

PREP DIRECTIONS

Combine the prep ingredients in a 1-gallon resealable freezer bag. Squeeze out the air, seal, label, and place in a round container to freeze into shape.

SERVING DAY DIRECTIONS

Add the stock and the contents of the package to the multi-cooker inner pot. Cook on high pressure for 7 minutes.

Let the pressure release naturally for 5 minutes, and then manually release any remaining pressure.

TEXAS-STYLE CHILI

Texas chili, often called Texas red, is packed with zesty spices, chopped vegetables, and fall-apart-tender cubes of meat. But don't dare try to add beans to this chili style! Chilis are so easy to make with the Fix 'n' Freeze method that you can try a new kind all the time—they're perfect for game days and busy family weeknights.

SERVES: 4 **PREP TIME:** 15 minutes **PRESSURE TIME:** 20 minutes **RELEASE METHOD:** Natural

PREP INGREDIENTS

- 2 pounds chuck roast, cut into 1-inch cubes
- 1 tablespoon minced canned chipotle pepper in adobo
- 1 onion, chopped
- 3 cloves garlic, chopped
- 1 jalapeño pepper, chopped, seeded if desired (optional)
- 2 tablespoons chili powder
- 1 teaspoon dried oregano
- 1 teaspoon ground cumin
- 1 tablespoon packed brown sugar
- 1 teaspoon salt
- 1 (14.5-ounce) can crushed tomatoes

SERVING DAY INGREDIENTS

- 1 cup chicken or beef stock

PREP DIRECTIONS

Combine the prep ingredients in a 1-gallon resealable freezer bag. Squeeze out the air, seal, label, and place in a round container to freeze into shape.

SERVING DAY DIRECTIONS

Add the stock and the contents of the package to the multi-cooker inner pot. Cook on high pressure for 20 minutes, and then let the pressure release naturally.

EASIEST VEGGIE CHILI EVER

The freezer-to-pressure-cooker method is an amazing time-saver. Other kitchen shortcuts can save you big on time without sacrificing taste as well. In this chili recipe, jarred salsa and roasted red peppers lend a hand. Serve topped with shredded cheese and chopped green onions.

SERVES: 4   **PREP TIME:** 10 minutes   **PRESSURE TIME:** 5 minutes   **RELEASE METHOD:** Natural (10 minutes)

PREP INGREDIENTS

- 2   (15.5-ounce) cans pinto or black beans, drained and rinsed
- 1   zucchini or yellow squash, halved lengthwise and cut into ½-inch-thick slices
- 1   tablespoon chili powder
- 1   (16-ounce) jar salsa
- 1   (6.7-ounce) jar sliced roasted red peppers, drained
- 2   tablespoons olive oil
  Salt to taste

SERVING DAY INGREDIENTS

- 1   cup vegetable stock

PREP DIRECTIONS

Combine the prep ingredients in a 1-gallon resealable freezer bag. Squeeze out the air, seal, label, and place in a round container to freeze into shape.

SERVING DAY DIRECTIONS

Add the stock and the contents of the package to the multi-cooker inner pot. Cook on high pressure for 5 minutes.

Let the pressure release naturally for 10 minutes, and then manually release any remaining pressure.

BLACK BEAN AND POBLANO CHILI

Fire-roasted tomatoes and poblano peppers lend a great mix of smoky and sweet to this vegetarian chili. If you would like to add meat, chorizo makes a good choice. Simply remove two links from the casings, cook them in a pan, breaking them into chunks, and let the meat cool before adding it to your freezer ingredients.

SERVES: 4   **PREP TIME:** 10 minutes   **PRESSURE TIME:** 7 minutes   **RELEASE METHOD:** Natural (5 minutes)

PREP INGREDIENTS

- 2 (15.5-ounce) cans black beans, drained and rinsed
- 1 (14.5-ounce) can fire-roasted whole tomatoes, drained
- 2 tablespoons olive oil
- 1 onion, chopped
- 2 poblano peppers, seeded and chopped
- 3 cloves garlic, minced
- 1 (16-ounce) jar tomatillo salsa (salsa verde)
-    Salt and pepper to taste

SERVING DAY INGREDIENTS

- 1 cup vegetable stock
-    Chopped fresh cilantro, for garnish (optional)

PREP DIRECTIONS

Combine the prep ingredients in a 1-gallon resealable freezer bag. Squeeze out the air, seal, label, and place in a round container to freeze into shape.

SERVING DAY DIRECTIONS

Add the stock and the contents of the package to the multi-cooker inner pot. Cook on high pressure for 7 minutes.

Let the pressure release naturally for 5 minutes, and then manually release any remaining pressure. If desired, garnish with chopped cilantro.

SWEET POTATO CHILI

This is not just another chili recipe! Sweet potato, beans, onion, tomatoes . . . how much nutrition can you pack into one delicious bowl? Adding soy sauce is a simple but clever kitchen twist to lend even more depth of flavor to this superfood supper. Even your traditional meat-eaters won't miss the meat.

SERVES: 4   **PREP TIME:** 15 minutes   **PRESSURE TIME:** 10 minutes   **RELEASE METHOD:** Natural (10 minutes)

PREP INGREDIENTS

- 1 sweet potato (about 1 pound), peeled and diced into ½-inch cubes
- 1 (15.5-ounce) can kidney beans or chickpeas, drained and rinsed
- 1 onion, chopped
- 3 cloves garlic, minced
- 1 (14.5-ounce) can diced tomatoes, drained
- 2 tablespoons chili powder
- 1 tablespoon soy sauce
- ½ teaspoon oregano
   Salt and pepper to taste

SERVING DAY INGREDIENTS

- 1 cup vegetable stock
- 1 (8.5-ounce) can corn, drained
- ¼ cup chopped fresh cilantro

PREP DIRECTIONS

Bring a medium pot of salted water to a boil over high heat. Add the sweet potato and blanch for 2 to 3 minutes. Drain and set aside in a single layer to cool. (A kitchen towel is useful for this task.)

Add the cooled potatoes and the remaining prep ingredients to a 1-gallon resealable freezer bag. Squeeze out the air, seal, label, and place in a round container to freeze into shape.

SERVING DAY DIRECTIONS

Add the stock and the contents of the package to the multi-cooker inner pot. Cook on high pressure for 10 minutes.

Let the pressure release naturally for 10 minutes, and then manually release any remaining pressure. Stir in the corn and chopped cilantro.

WHITE CHICKEN CHILI

"Classic" chili may bring to mind beef and kidney beans, but this flavorful white chili recipe will become just as much a classic in your kitchen once you give it a try. If you want to tone down the spice, simply swap in cubanelles (Italian frying peppers) or green bell peppers for the poblano peppers.

SERVES: 4 to 6   **PREP TIME:** 15 minutes   **PRESSURE TIME:** 8 minutes   **RELEASE METHOD:** Natural (10 minutes)

PREP INGREDIENTS

1½ pounds boneless, skinless chicken thighs, cut into 1½-inch pieces

2 (14.5-ounce) cans white beans, such as cannellini or Great Northern, drained and rinsed

1 jalapeño pepper, seeded and diced (optional)

2 poblano peppers, seeded and chopped

1 onion, chopped

3 cloves garlic, minced

2 teaspoons ground cumin

1 teaspoon dried oregano

Salt and pepper to taste

SERVING DAY INGREDIENTS

1 cup chicken stock

2-3 tablespoons chopped cilantro or parsley

PREP DIRECTIONS

Combine the prep ingredients in a 1-gallon resealable freezer bag. Squeeze out the air, seal, label, and place in a round container to freeze into shape.

SERVING DAY DIRECTIONS

Add the stock and the contents of the package to the multi-cooker inner pot. Cook on high pressure for 8 minutes.

Let the pressure release naturally for 10 minutes, and then manually release any remaining pressure. Stir in the cilantro.

SANDWICHES & TACOS

CLASSIC SLOPPY JOES

A family favorite becomes lightning fast to get on the table when you prep and freeze ahead. Classic Sloppy Joes are so versatile to have on hand and easy to customize to your dinner companions' liking. For a little spice, add a dash of hot sauce, such as Sriracha, to the prep ingredients. Want to sneak in a vegetable? Add a finely chopped bell pepper to the prep bag. What Sloppy Joe special order will be on the menu this week?

SERVES: 4　　**PREP TIME:** 15 minutes　　**PRESSURE TIME:** 7 minutes　　**RELEASE METHOD:** Natural (5 minutes)

PREP INGREDIENTS

- 1½ pounds ground beef or turkey, browned, drained, and cooled
- 1 small onion, chopped
- 2 cloves garlic, chopped
- ¾ cup ketchup
- 1 tablespoon Worcestershire sauce
- 1 tablespoon yellow or Dijon mustard
- 1 tablespoon packed brown sugar
  Salt to taste

SERVING DAY INGREDIENTS

- 1 cup chicken stock
- 4 hamburger buns

PREP DIRECTIONS

Combine the prep ingredients in a 1-gallon resealable freezer bag. Squeeze out the air, seal, label, and place in a round container to freeze into shape.

SERVING DAY DIRECTIONS

Add the stock and the contents of the package to the multi-cooker inner pot. Cook on high pressure for 7 minutes.

Let the pressure release naturally for 5 minutes, and then manually release any remaining pressure. Turn the pot to Sauté and simmer to thicken the sauce if desired. Serve on hamburger buns.

BARBECUE CHICKEN SLIDERS

Using chicken thighs keeps this dish super moist, delicious, and economical. Top the tender results with coleslaw or shredded cabbage, or get spicy with a topping of pepper Jack cheese. To stretch the dinner possibilities, skip the buns and serve the saucy chicken over rice. However your family enjoys it, you'll appreciate how quickly this dinner is ready for your table!

SERVES: 4   **PREP TIME:** 15 minutes   **PRESSURE TIME:** 10 minutes   **RELEASE METHOD:** Natural (5 minutes)

PREP INGREDIENTS

- 2 pounds boneless, skinless chicken thighs, cut into 1½-inch pieces
- 1 small onion, chopped
- 3 cloves garlic, minced
- 1 cup ketchup
- ½ cup apple cider vinegar
- ½ cup packed brown sugar
- 2 tablespoons Worcestershire sauce
- 1 tablespoon hot sauce
- 2 teaspoons dry mustard

SERVING DAY INGREDIENTS

- 1¼ cups chicken stock
- 8 slider buns

PREP DIRECTIONS

Combine the prep ingredients in a 1-gallon resealable freezer bag. Squeeze out the air, seal, label, and place in a round container to freeze into shape.

SERVING DAY DIRECTIONS

Add the stock and contents of the package to the multi-cooker inner pot. Cook on high pressure for 10 minutes.

Let the pressure release naturally for 5 minutes, and then manually release any remaining pressure.

Using a slotted spoon, transfer the chicken to a large bowl and shred it using two forks. Meanwhile, turn the pot to Sauté and reduce the liquid, stirring frequently, to the desired consistency.

Add the sauce to the chicken and toss to coat evenly. Serve on slider buns.

LOADED CHEESESTEAK SANDWICHES

Chopped steak, luscious peppers and onions, and melted provolone cheese . . . take your order to your freezer instead of the local sub shop! With the Fix 'n' Freeze method, your pressure cooker does the work while you save money and savor the results. Prefer crisper peppers? Omit them from the prep bag and add them when the beef is finished, cooking for a few minutes until softened.

SERVES: 6   **PREP TIME:** 10 minutes   **PRESSURE TIME:** 20 minutes   **RELEASE METHOD:** Natural

PREP INGREDIENTS

2   pounds blade steak, cut into 2-inch pieces (be sure to remove the center gristle in each steak)

1   (0.7-ounce) packet Italian dressing mix

1   onion, halved and sliced

2   green or red bell peppers, seeded and sliced

2   tablespoons tomato paste

Salt and pepper to taste

SERVING DAY INGREDIENTS

1   cup beef stock

6   steak rolls

6   slices provolone cheese

PREP DIRECTIONS

Combine the prep ingredients in a 1-gallon resealable freezer bag. Squeeze out the air, seal, label, and place in a round container to freeze into shape.

SERVING DAY DIRECTIONS

Add the stock and the contents of the package to the multi-cooker inner pot. Cook on high pressure for 20 minutes.

Let the pressure release naturally. If desired, shred the beef with two forks. Serve on rolls topped with a slice of provolone cheese. To melt the cheese, you can stick the sandwiches under the broiler for 1 to 2 minutes.

FRENCH DIP SANDWICHES

Thinly sliced beef on a crusty roll with juice on the side for dipping. It's not just a restaurant order; it can be dinner from your freezer any time you crave it. Serve topped with provolone or Swiss cheese. Putting the sandwiches under the broiler for just a minute or two will melt the cheese and toast the roll.

SERVES: 4 to 6   **PREP TIME:** 10 minutes   **PRESSURE TIME:** 20 minutes   **RELEASE METHOD:** Natural

PREP INGREDIENTS

2   pounds chuck roast, thinly sliced

2   large onions, thinly sliced

3   cloves garlic, minced

1   tablespoon olive oil

1   tablespoon Worcestershire sauce

1   (1-ounce) packet French onion soup mix

½   teaspoon ground thyme
     Salt and pepper to taste

SERVING DAY INGREDIENTS

1   cup beef stock

4   to 6 steak rolls

PREP DIRECTIONS

Combine the prep ingredients in a 1-gallon resealable freezer bag. Squeeze out the air, seal, label, and place in a round container to freeze into shape.

SERVING DAY DIRECTIONS

Add the stock and the contents of the package to the multi-cooker inner pot. Cook on high pressure for 20 minutes, and then let the pressure release naturally. Serve on rolls, with small bowls of the juice for dipping.

CHICKEN TINGA

This dish of shredded chicken in a roasted tomato-chipotle sauce is a crowd-pleaser that's easy to make on weeknights and impressive enough for company. It's delicious on its own or served on corn tortillas with sliced avocado and crumbled Mexican cheese, such as cotija.

SERVES: 4 to 6   **PREP TIME:** 15 minutes   **PRESSURE TIME:** 8 minutes   **RELEASE METHOD:** Natural (10 minutes)

PREP INGREDIENTS

- 2   pounds boneless, skinless chicken thighs, cut into 1-inch pieces
- 1   onion, chopped
- 3   cloves garlic, minced
- ½   cup jarred tomatillo salsa
- ½   (15-ounce) can fire-roasted tomatoes
- 1   tablespoon minced canned chipotle pepper in adobo
- 1   tablespoon Worcestershire sauce
- 1   teaspoon dried oregano
      Salt and pepper to taste

SERVING DAY INGREDIENTS

- 1   cup chicken stock

PREP DIRECTIONS

Combine the prep ingredients in a 1-gallon resealable freezer bag. Squeeze out the air, seal, label, and place in a round container to freeze into shape.

SERVING DAY DIRECTIONS

Add the stock and the contents of the package to the multi-cooker inner pot. Cook on high pressure for 8 minutes.

Let the pressure release naturally for 10 minutes, and then manually release any remaining pressure.

BEER-BRAISED TURKEY TACOS

Beer is the not-so-secret ingredient that makes this recipe outstanding. Serve the super-tender turkey and accompaniments on either hard or soft shell tacos. Finish off with your favorite taco toppings, which may include a little cheese, sour cream, diced tomato, and shredded lettuce.

SERVES: 4 to 6   **PREP TIME:** 10 minutes   **PRESSURE TIME:** 8 minutes   **RELEASE METHOD:** Natural (10 minutes)

PREP INGREDIENTS

- 2 pounds boneless, skinless turkey breast, cut into 2-inch pieces
- 1 jalapeño pepper, chopped, seeded if desired (optional)
- 1 (8-ounce) can tomato sauce
- 1 (4.5-ounce) can green chiles
- 1 tablespoon Worcestershire sauce
- 2 tablespoons chili powder
  Salt and pepper to taste

SERVING DAY INGREDIENTS

- ½ cup beer
- ½ cup chicken stock
- 4–6 taco shells or corn tortillas

PREP DIRECTIONS

Combine the prep ingredients in a 1-gallon resealable freezer bag. Squeeze out the air, seal, label, and place in a round container to freeze into shape.

SERVING DAY DIRECTIONS

Add the beer, the stock, and the contents of the package to the multi-cooker inner pot. Cook on high pressure for 8 minutes.

Let the pressure release naturally for 10 minutes, and then manually release any remaining pressure. Shred the turkey with two forks.

TURKEY AND BLACK BEAN BURRITOS

Dinner is a wrap when you have the fillings for these hearty burritos ready to go from freezer to pressure cooker. Ten minutes is all it takes—and might be all you have to spare on a weeknight. Complete the dinner with a toppings bar (think: cheese, avocado, lettuce, and sour cream) and side salads.

SERVES: 4   **PREP TIME:** 10 minutes   **PRESSURE TIME:** 5 minutes   **RELEASE METHOD:** Natural (5 minutes)

PREP INGREDIENTS

- 1   tablespoon olive oil
- 1   pound ground turkey
- 1   (1-ounce) package taco seasoning mix
- 1   (15.5-ounce) can black beans, rinsed and drained
- 1   cup jarred salsa
- ¼   cup chopped fresh cilantro

SERVING DAY INGREDIENTS

- 1   cup chicken stock
- 4   flour tortillas

PREP DIRECTIONS

Heat the olive oil in a medium nonstick skillet over medium heat. Add the turkey and cook, breaking up large chunks with a wooden spoon, until browned. Drain any excess fat. Add the taco seasoning and water, according to package instructions. Cook until the mixture is slightly reduced and thickened, 3 to 5 minutes. Set aside to cool.

Add the turkey, along the with the remaining prep ingredients, to a 1-gallon resealable freezer bag. Squeeze out the air, seal, label, and place in a round container to freeze into shape.

SERVING DAY DIRECTIONS

Add the stock and the contents of the package to the multi-cooker inner pot. Cook on high pressure for 5 minutes.

Let the pressure release naturally for 5 minutes, and then release any remaining pressure. Portion into flour tortillas, add toppings of your choice and roll up.

SHREDDED BEEF TACOS

Fork-tender beef is a tasty taco meat alternative to ground beef. And skip the seasoning packet—you can create your own spice mixture quickly without the cost and preservatives in store-bought. Serve in taco shells or on tortillas with your favorite toppings.

SERVES: 4 to 6   **PREP TIME:** 15 minutes   **PRESSURE TIME:** 15 minutes   **RELEASE METHOD:** Natural (10 minutes)

PREP INGREDIENTS

- 2 pounds chuck roast, cut into 1-inch cubes
- 1 onion, chopped
- 1 red or green bell pepper, seeded and chopped
- 1 (10-ounce) can diced tomatoes with green chiles
- 1 tablespoon olive oil
- 2 tablespoons chili powder
- 1 teaspoon smoked paprika
- ½ teaspoon dried oregano
  Salt and pepper to taste

SERVING DAY INGREDIENTS

- 1 cup chicken or beef stock
  Taco shells or tortillas

PREP DIRECTIONS

Combine the prep ingredients in a 1-gallon resealable freezer bag. Squeeze out the air, seal, label, and place in a round container to freeze into shape.

SERVING DAY DIRECTIONS

Add the stock and the contents of the package to the multi-cooker inner pot. Cook on high pressure for 15 minutes.

Let the pressure release naturally for 10 minutes, and then manually release any remaining pressure. Shred the beef with two forks.

CHIPOTLE CARNITAS

With your pressure cooker, tender shredded pork can be on your dinner table faster than making a run to the local taco shop. Warm up some corn tortillas and serve carnitas topped with chopped cilantro and a squeeze of lime juice.

SERVES: 4   **PREP TIME:** 15 minutes   **PRESSURE TIME:** 15 minutes   **RELEASE METHOD:** Natural

PREP INGREDIENTS

- 2   pounds pork shoulder or butt, cut into 1-inch cubes
- 4   cloves garlic, minced
- 1   canned chile in adobo, chopped
- 2   teaspoons dried oregano
- 1½   teaspoons salt
- 1   teaspoon black pepper
- ¼   cup orange juice

SERVING DAY INGREDIENTS

- 1   cup chicken or beef stock
- 4   corn tortillas
       Juice of ½ lime
- ¼   cup chopped cilantro

PREP DIRECTIONS

Combine the prep ingredients in a 1-gallon resealable freezer bag. Squeeze out the air, seal, label, and place in a round container to freeze into shape.

SERVING DAY DIRECTIONS

Add the stock and the contents of the package to the multi-cooker inner pot. Cook on high pressure for 15 minutes.

Let the pressure release naturally. When cool enough to handle, shred the pork with two forks. If you prefer your carnitas crispy, transfer the meat to a large skillet. Cook over medium-high heat, stirring regularly, until the edges are crispy and browned in spots. Top with the lime juice and chopped cilantro. Serve in corn tortillas.

STREET TACOS

Inspired by tacos al pastor, a Central Mexican–style taco, this dish features tender chunks of pork melded with pineapple and chile seasoning. Serve on warmed corn tortillas with your favorite toppings; try chopped onion, cilantro, lime juice, sour cream, and avocado chunks.

SERVES: 4 to 6　**PREP TIME:** 15 minutes　**PRESSURE TIME:** 25 minutes　**RELEASE METHOD:** Natural (10 minutes)

PREP INGREDIENTS

- 2　pounds pork shoulder, cut into 1-inch cubes
- ½　onion, chopped
- 3　cloves garlic, crushed
- ¼　cup crushed canned pineapple
- 2　tablespoons ancho chile powder
- 2　teaspoons chopped canned chipotle pepper in adobo
- ½　teaspoon ground cumin
- ½　teaspoon dried oregano
- 1　tablespoon vinegar
- 　Salt to taste

SERVING DAY INGREDIENTS

- 1　cup chicken stock
- 4-6　corn tortillas

PREP DIRECTIONS

Combine the prep ingredients in a 1-gallon resealable freezer bag. Squeeze out the air, seal, label, and place in a round container to freeze into shape.

SERVING DAY DIRECTIONS

Add the stock and the contents of the package to the multi-cooker inner pot. Cook on high pressure for 25 minutes.

Let the pressure release naturally for 10 minutes, and then manually release any remaining pressure. Using a slotted spoon, transfer the pork to a bowl and shred with two forks.

Meanwhile, turn the pot to Sauté and reduce the liquid, stirring frequently, until it's like a glaze, about 10 minutes. Add some of the sauce to the pork and toss to coat. Serve on warmed corn tortillas.

PASTA

SHORT RIB RAGU

No more stress when dinner guests drop in! Any ordinary pasta becomes company-worthy when topped with this beefy and bold sauce. Keep a package of the prep ingredients ready in your freezer at all times to whip up an impressive meal for special dinner companions or to simply treat your family any night of the week. A fresh green salad makes the perfect side.

SERVES: 4   **PREP TIME:** 10 minutes   **PRESSURE TIME:** 20 minutes   **RELEASE METHOD:** Natural

PREP INGREDIENTS

1   pound boneless beef short ribs, cut into 1-inch pieces

2   (28-ounce) cans crushed tomatoes

2   tablespoons tomato paste

1   onion, chopped

4   cloves garlic, minced

2   teaspoons dried oregano

1   teaspoon sugar

     Salt and pepper to taste

SERVING DAY INGREDIENTS

½   cup dry red wine

½   cup beef stock

     Pasta of your choice, cooked according to package directions

PREP DIRECTIONS

Combine the prep ingredients in a 1-gallon resealable freezer bag. Squeeze out the air, seal, label, and place in a round container to freeze into shape.

SERVING DAY DIRECTIONS

Add the wine, the stock, and the contents of the package to the multi-cooker inner pot. Cook on high pressure for 20 minutes.

Let the pressure release naturally. Serve over the pasta of your choice.

BOLOGNESE SAUCE

This hearty Italian meat sauce usually requires hours of stovetop simmering. Now, you can enjoy the rich sauce and its incredible aroma in just minutes with your pressure cooker. It's a quick warm-up for cold winter nights. Serve over your favorite pasta.

SERVES: 4   **PREP TIME:** 15 minutes   **PRESSURE TIME:** 7 minutes   **RELEASE METHOD:** Natural

PREP INGREDIENTS

1   pound ground beef, browned, drained, and cooled

1   (28-ounce) can crushed tomatoes

2   tablespoons tomato paste

½   cup dry white wine

1   rib celery, diced

1   carrot, peeled and diced

1   small onion, chopped

4   cloves garlic, minced

2   tablespoons dehydrated minced onion

1   teaspoon dried oregano

1   teaspoon dried basil

Salt to taste

SERVING DAY INGREDIENTS

1   cup beef stock

Pasta of your choice, cooked according to package directions

PREP DIRECTIONS

Combine the prep ingredients in a 1-gallon resealable freezer bag. Squeeze out the air, seal, label, and place in a round container to freeze into shape.

SERVING DAY DIRECTIONS

Add the stock and the contents of the package to the multi-cooker inner pot. Cook on high pressure for 7 minutes.

Let the pressure release naturally. Serve over the pasta of your choice.

LENTIL BOLOGNESE

Looking for a lighter, meatless way to satisfy your craving for Italian comfort food? Lentils and mushrooms give so much hearty flavor to this sauce that you won't even miss the meat. Serve over pasta and garnish with torn basil leaves, if desired.

SERVES: 4   **PREP TIME:** 10 minutes   **PRESSURE TIME:** 12 minutes   **RELEASE METHOD:** Natural

PREP INGREDIENTS

- 1   cup dried red lentils, picked over for debris and rinsed
- 1   onion, finely chopped
- 1   carrot, peeled and chopped
- 2   cloves garlic, minced
-      Handful dried porcini mushrooms (optional)
- 2   tablespoons tomato paste
- 2   teaspoons soy sauce
- 1   (14.5-ounce) can crushed tomatoes
- 1   tablespoon Italian seasoning
-      Salt and pepper to taste

SERVING DAY INGREDIENTS

- 1   cup vegetable stock
-      Pasta of your choice, cooked according to package directions
-      Torn basil leaves, for garnish (optional)

PREP DIRECTIONS

Combine the prep ingredients in a 1-gallon resealable freezer bag. Squeeze out the air, seal, label, and place in a round container to freeze into shape.

SERVING DAY DIRECTIONS

Add the stock and the contents of the package to the multi-cooker inner pot. Cook on high pressure for 12 minutes.

Let the pressure release naturally. Serve over the pasta of your choice.

SPINACH LASAGNA

The Fix 'n' Freeze method that calls for advance prep can save you a lot of time with fussy dishes like lasagna. The flavor will be just as fabulous. Just make sure you note that, unlike most of the other recipes in this book, the lasagna must be thawed in the refrigerator before cooking to avoid frozen spots.

SERVES: 4 to 6   **PREP TIME:** 25 minutes   **PRESSURE TIME:** 20 minutes   **RELEASE METHOD:** Natural (10 minutes)

PREP INGREDIENTS

- 1   (16-ounce) bag frozen chopped spinach, thawed and drained
- 1   egg, lightly beaten
- 8   ounces shredded mozzarella cheese, divided
- 1   (15-ounce) container ricotta cheese
- ½   cup grated Parmesan cheese
      Pinch of ground nutmeg (optional)
- ¼   teaspoon salt
- ½   teaspoon black pepper
- 1   (25-ounce) jar tomato sauce (you may not need it all)
- 1   (9-ounce) package no-boil lasagna noodles (you may not need them all)

SERVING DAY INGREDIENTS

1½   cups water

PREP DIRECTIONS

In a medium bowl, stir together the drained spinach, egg, two-thirds of the mozzarella, ricotta, Parmesan, nutmeg (if using), salt, and pepper.

Spread a thin layer of sauce over the bottom of a 7-inch springform pan. Break up the uncooked lasagna noodles and place them in a single layer on the bottom of the pan. Spread a layer of the spinach-cheese mixture, then a layer of sauce. Top with another layer of noodles broken to fit. Continue layering, ending with a final layer of noodles and sauce. Top with the remaining one-third mozzarella cheese. Cover tightly with aluminum foil and freeze.

SERVING DAY DIRECTIONS

Thaw completely in the refrigerator. Add the water and the trivet to the bottom of the multi-cooker. Using a foil sling, gently lower the covered lasagna onto the trivet. Tuck in the foil ends and cook on high pressure for 20 minutes.

Let the pressure release naturally for 10 minutes, and then manually release any remaining pressure. Check for doneness, adding more time if necessary.

If desired, transfer the uncovered lasagna to the oven and broil for a few minutes until the cheese is golden brown. Let rest for 15 minutes before releasing from the springform pan and slicing.

SAUSAGE LASAGNA

You can rest easy knowing there is a luscious lasagna in your freezer waiting to be called to the dinner table when you need it. But plan ahead for that rescue meal: unlike most of the other recipes in this book, the lasagna must be thawed in the refrigerator before cooking to avoid frozen spots.

SERVES: 4 to 6 **PREP TIME:** 25 minutes **PRESSURE TIME:** 20 minutes **RELEASE METHOD:** Natural (10 minutes)

PREP INGREDIENTS

- 1 egg, lightly beaten
- 8 ounces shredded mozzarella cheese, divided
- 1 (15-ounce) container ricotta cheese
- ½ cup grated Parmesan cheese
  Pinch of ground nutmeg (optional)
  Salt and pepper to taste
- 1 (25-ounce) jar tomato sauce
- 1 (9-ounce) package no-boil lasagna noodles (you may not need them all)
- 1 pound bulk Italian sausage meat (sweet or hot), browned, drained, and cooled

SERVING DAY INGREDIENTS

1½ cups water

PREP DIRECTIONS

In a medium bowl, stir together the egg, two-thirds of the mozzarella, ricotta, Parmesan, nutmeg (if using), and salt and pepper.

Spread a thin layer of sauce over the bottom of a 7-inch springform pan. Break up the uncooked lasagna noodles and place them in a single layer on the bottom of the pan. Spread a layer of cooled sausage, then a layer of the cheese mixture, then a layer of sauce. Top with another layer of noodles broken to fit. Continue layering, ending with a final layer of noodles and sauce. Top with the remaining one-third mozzarella cheese. Cover tightly with aluminum foil and freeze.

SERVING DAY DIRECTIONS

Thaw the lasagna completely in the refrigerator.

Add the water and the trivet to the bottom of the multi-cooker. Using a foil sling, gently lower the covered lasagna onto the trivet. Tuck in the foil ends and cook on high pressure for 20 minutes.

Let the pressure release naturally for 10 minutes, and then manually release any remaining pressure. Check for doneness, adding more time if necessary.

If desired, transfer the uncovered lasagna to the oven and broil for a few minutes until the cheese is golden brown. Let rest for 15 minutes before releasing from the springform pan and slicing.

CHILI MAC AND CHEESE

It's a cheesy, meaty mashup of two family favorites in this dish that goes from pressure cooker to dinner table in less than 20 minutes. Boiling the macaroni while the pressure releases is a smart time-saver that helps you bring it all together as quickly as possible and enjoy the good stuff sooner.

SERVES: 4   **PREP TIME:** 15 minutes   **PRESSURE TIME:** 7 minutes   **RELEASE METHOD:** Natural (10 minutes)

PREP INGREDIENTS

- 1 pound ground beef, browned, drained, and cooled
- 1 onion, chopped
- 3 cloves garlic, minced
- 1 (14.5-ounce) can diced tomatoes
- 1 (4.5-ounce) can green chiles
- 1 (15.5-ounce) can kidney beans, drained and rinsed
- 2 tablespoons chili powder
  Salt and pepper to taste

SERVING DAY INGREDIENTS

- 1 cup chicken or beef stock
- 2 cups dried macaroni
- 1 cup shredded cheese (such as Cheddar, Monterey Jack, or pepper Jack)
- ¼ cup chopped fresh cilantro

PREP DIRECTIONS

Combine the prep ingredients in a 1-gallon resealable freezer bag. Squeeze out the air, seal, label, and place in a round container to freeze into shape.

SERVING DAY DIRECTIONS

Add the stock and the contents of the package to the multi-cooker inner pot. Cook on high pressure for 7 minutes.

Let the pressure release naturally for 10 minutes, and then manually release any remaining pressure.

Meanwhile, on the stovetop, bring a large pot of salted water to a boil, add the macaroni, and cook, stirring occasionally, until tender. Drain, and stir into the chili, along with the cheese and cilantro.

SHRIMP SCAMPI

Don't wait to dine out to enjoy shrimp scampi! This Fix 'n' Freeze version of the dish tastes amazing and only calls for 1 minute of cooking time. It's true! In fact, it's key to use frozen shrimp so it doesn't overcook. Serve over pasta.

SERVES: 4   **PREP TIME:** 5 minutes   **PRESSURE TIME:** 1 minute   **RELEASE METHOD:** Manual

PREP INGREDIENTS

- 2 pounds frozen peeled and deveined shrimp
- 5 cloves garlic, minced
- ¼ cup minced fresh parsley
  Salt and pepper to taste
- ¼ cup dry white wine

SERVING DAY INGREDIENTS

- 1 cup chicken stock
- 1 tablespoon lemon juice
- 4 tablespoons unsalted butter

PREP DIRECTIONS

Keep the shrimp frozen separately from the other ingredients. Combine the remaining prep ingredients in a small resealable freezer bag. Squeeze out the air, seal, label, and freeze.

SERVING DAY DIRECTIONS

Add the stock, the shrimp, and the contents of the package to the multi-cooker inner pot. Cook on high pressure for 1 minute.

Manually release the pressure. Using a slotted spoon, transfer the shrimp to a bowl. Turn the pot to Sauté and simmer the sauce until slightly thickened, 2 to 3 minutes, and then stir in the lemon juice and butter. Toss the shrimp with the sauce.

CHICKEN & TURKEY

CLASSIC BUFFALO WINGS

Just keep a bag of frozen wings in the freezer, and you're ready to serve guests! If you prefer to freeze fresh wings, cut each whole wing into two pieces, discarding the wing tip. To prevent the wings from freezing into a giant block, place the wings on a lined baking sheet and freeze. Once they are frozen, you can transfer them to a resealable freezer bag. Serve with blue cheese and celery.

SERVES: 4 to 6   **PRESSURE TIME:** 8 minutes   **RELEASE METHOD:** Natural (10 minutes)

PREP INGREDIENTS

24 frozen chicken wings
    (see headnote)

SERVING DAY INGREDIENTS

1   cup water

6   tablespoons unsalted butter, melted

⅓   cup hot sauce

1   clove garlic, minced

SERVING DAY DIRECTIONS

Add the water and the trivet to the inner pot of the multi-cooker. Place the wings on top of the trivet. Cook on high pressure for 8 minutes.

Let the pressure release naturally for 10 minutes, and then manually release any remaining pressure. Meanwhile, in a large bowl, stir together the melted butter, hot sauce, and minced garlic.

Set the oven to broil. Transfer the wings to a nonstick baking sheet and brush lightly with the sauce. Transfer the baking sheet to the broiler and broil until light golden brown and crispy. Flip, brush the other side with the sauce, and return to the broiler. Carefully transfer the crispy wings to the bowl and toss with the remaining sauce.

HONEY-MUSTARD WINGS

Don't save wings as a special treat for only game days! You can have wings whenever you want with this easy method. Mixing up the sauce while the wings are in the multi-cooker saves time, so you're ready to brush, broil, and enjoy the crispy, golden brown, delicious results.

SERVES: 4 to 6   **PRESSURE TIME:** 8 minutes   **RELEASE METHOD:** Natural (10 minutes)

PREP INGREDIENTS

24 frozen chicken wings (see headnote, page 109)

SERVING DAY INGREDIENTS

1   cup water

4   tablespoons unsalted butter, melted

⅓   cup spicy brown or Dijon mustard

¼   cup honey

1   clove garlic, minced

SERVING DAY DIRECTIONS

Add the water and the trivet to the inner pot of the multi-cooker. Place the wings on top of the trivet. Cook on high pressure for 8 minutes.

Let the pressure release naturally for 10 minutes, and then manually release any remaining pressure. Meanwhile, in a large bowl, stir together the melted butter, mustard, honey, and garlic. You can add more mustard or honey to taste.

Set the oven to broil. Transfer the wings to a nonstick baking sheet and brush lightly with the sauce. Transfer the baking sheet to the broiler and broil until light golden brown and crispy. Flip, brush the other side with the sauce, and return to the broiler. Carefully transfer the crispy wings to the bowl and toss with the remaining sauce.

COUNTRY CAPTAIN

Popular in the South, country captain is a curried chicken dish packed with flavor. In fact, the name is said to have originated back in the days when ship captains in southern ports traded in spices they brought back from overseas travels. All you need to do is go to your freezer to pull out the prepped ingredients.

SERVES: 4   **PREP TIME:** 15 minutes   **PRESSURE TIME:** 8 minutes   **RELEASE METHOD:** Natural (10 minutes)

PREP INGREDIENTS

2   pounds boneless, skinless chicken thighs, cut into 2-inch pieces

1   medium onion, chopped

1   green bell pepper, seeded and chopped

1   cup canned diced tomatoes

1   tablespoon curry powder

½   teaspoon ground thyme

¼   cup raisins or currants

     Salt and pepper to taste

SERVING DAY INGREDIENTS

1   cup chicken stock

¼   cup slivered or sliced almonds

PREP DIRECTIONS

Combine the prep ingredients in a 1-gallon resealable freezer bag. Squeeze out the air, seal, label, and place in a round container to freeze into shape.

SERVING DAY DIRECTIONS

Add the stock and the contents of the package to the multi-cooker inner pot. Cook on high pressure for 8 minutes.

Let the pressure release naturally for 10 minutes, and then manually release any remaining pressure. If the sauce is too thin, transfer the chicken to a plate, turn the pot to Sauté, and simmer until the sauce reaches the desired consistency. Garnish with the almonds.

HONEY-MUSTARD CHICKEN DRUMSTICKS

Sweet, tangy, and delicious—this will become the only way you want your chicken drumsticks! Keep a batch of the sauce on call at all times in your freezer. To get beautifully bronzed and crispy skin, stick the drumsticks under the broiler for a few minutes.

SERVES: 4   **PREP TIME:** 5 minutes   **PRESSURE TIME:** 15 minutes   **RELEASE METHOD:** Natural (10 minutes)

PREP INGREDIENTS

- ⅓ cup whole-grain mustard
- ½ cup honey
- 2 tablespoons apple cider vinegar
- 1 tablespoon soy sauce
- ½ teaspoon salt
- ¼ teaspoon pepper
- 2 pounds chicken drumsticks

SERVING DAY INGREDIENTS

- 1 cup chicken stock

PREP DIRECTIONS

In a small freezer container, stir together the mustard, honey, vinegar, soy sauce, salt, and pepper. Seal tightly and freeze. In a large resealable freezer bag, add the chicken drumsticks and seal. Place them on a large freezer-safe pan so that they lie flat and freeze individually. You may need to use more than one bag.

SERVING DAY DIRECTIONS

Add the stock, the chicken, and the contents of the sauce container to the multi-cooker inner pot. Cook on high pressure for 15 minutes.

Let the pressure release naturally for 10 minutes, and then manually release any remaining pressure.

Transfer the chicken to a serving dish. If desired, crisp up the skin for a few minutes under the broiler. Meanwhile, reduce the sauce, stirring occasionally, until it's the consistency of a glaze. Spoon the glaze over the chicken.

BOURBON CHICKEN

Named after Bourbon Street in New Orleans, this popular Cajun-Chinese dish is the perfect mix of sweet and savory. Although the flavor is complex, the ingredients are simple items you're likely to have on hand in your kitchen. Serve over rice.

SERVES: 4   **PREP TIME:** 15 minutes   **PRESSURE TIME:** 8 minutes   **RELEASE METHOD:** Natural (10 minutes)

PREP INGREDIENTS

- 2   pounds boneless, skinless chicken thighs, cut into 1-inch pieces
- ½   onion, chopped
- 2   teaspoons minced fresh ginger
- 3   cloves garlic, minced
-     Pinch of crushed red pepper flakes (optional)
- ½   cup soy sauce
- ½   cup packed light or dark brown sugar
- 2   tablespoons ketchup
- 1   tablespoon rice vinegar

SERVING DAY INGREDIENTS

- ¼   cup apple juice
- ¾   cup chicken stock
- 2   tablespoons cornstarch
- 3   tablespoons cold water

PREP DIRECTIONS

Combine the prep ingredients in a 1-gallon resealable freezer bag. Squeeze out the air, seal, label, and place in a round container to freeze into shape.

SERVING DAY DIRECTIONS

Add the apple juice, the chicken stock, and the contents of the package to the multi-cooker inner pot. Cook on high pressure for 8 minutes.

Let the pressure release naturally for 10 minutes, and then release any remaining pressure.

In a small bowl, stir together the cornstarch and water. Set the pot to Sauté, and stir in the cornstarch mixture until the sauce is slightly thickened.

KUNG PAO CHICKEN

You'll love this recipe that's quicker and healthier than takeout. If you want additional vegetables, feel free to throw a few handfuls of fresh or frozen veggies in at the end before adding the cornstarch mixture. Cook them for a few minutes just until they're crisp-tender.

SERVES: 4 to 6   **PREP TIME:** 15 minutes   **PRESSURE TIME:** 10 minutes   **RELEASE METHOD:** Natural (5 minutes)

PREP INGREDIENTS

- 2   pounds boneless, skinless chicken thighs, cut into 1½-inch pieces
- 1   red bell pepper, seeded and chopped
- 1   onion, chopped
- 3   cloves garlic, minced
- 1   tablespoon minced ginger
- 1   tablespoon white vinegar
- 2   tablespoons hoisin sauce
- 1   tablespoon Sriracha sauce

SERVING DAY INGREDIENTS

- ¾   cup chicken stock
- ¼   cup soy sauce
- 2   tablespoons cornstarch
- 3   tablespoons cold water
- ¼   cup coarsely chopped peanuts
- 2   green onions, thinly sliced
- 1   teaspoon sesame oil (optional)

PREP DIRECTIONS

Combine the prep ingredients in a 1-gallon resealable freezer bag. Squeeze out the air, seal, label, and place in a round container to freeze into shape.

SERVING DAY DIRECTIONS

Add the stock, the soy sauce, and the contents of the package to the multi-cooker inner pot. Cook on high pressure for 10 minutes.

Let the pressure release naturally for 5 minutes, and then manually release any remaining pressure. Meanwhile, in a small bowl, mix together the cornstarch and water.

Set the pot to Sauté, and stir in the cornstarch mixture until the sauce is slightly thickened. Stir in the peanuts, green onions, and sesame oil (if using).

SWEET AND SOUR CHICKEN

You can enjoy the delicious flavor medley of chicken, pineapple, and bell pepper any time, without a run to a restaurant. For an even more gourmet touch, add fresh snow peas at the end and let them cook for a minute or two. Serve over rice.

SERVES: 4   **PREP TIME:** 15 minutes   **PRESSURE TIME:** 8 minutes   **RELEASE METHOD:** Natural (10 minutes)

PREP INGREDIENTS

- 1½ pounds boneless, skinless chicken thighs, cut into 1-inch pieces
- 2 bell peppers, seeded and cut into 1-inch chunks
- 1 onion, cut into 1-inch chunks
- 1 (10-ounce) can pineapple chunks, drained
- 1 teaspoon ground ginger
- 3 tablespoons white or apple cider vinegar
- 2 tablespoons soy sauce
- 1 tablespoon canola oil
- ¼ cup packed brown sugar
- 3 tablespoons ketchup
   Salt to taste

SERVING DAY INGREDIENTS

- 1 cup chicken stock
- 2 tablespoons cornstarch
- 3 tablespoons cold water
- 1 cup snow peas (optional)

PREP DIRECTIONS

Combine the prep ingredients in a 1-gallon resealable freezer bag. Squeeze out the air, seal, label, and place in a round container to freeze into shape.

SERVING DAY DIRECTIONS

Add the stock and the contents of the package to the multi-cooker inner pot. Cook on high pressure for 8 minutes.

Let the pressure release naturally for 10 minutes, and then manually release any remaining pressure. In a small bowl, stir together the cornstarch and water. Set the pot to Sauté, and stir in the cornstarch mixture until the sauce is slightly thickened. If desired, when you add the cornstarch, you can also stir in the snow peas.

GARLIC-GINGER CHICKEN AND BROCCOLI

This chicken dish is a family favorite that is often prepared by stir-frying. But calling your pressure cooker in to do the cooking makes it an even quicker option with very little hands-on time required. Adding the broccoli at the end for just a few minutes keeps it crisp-tender.

SERVES: 4 **PREP TIME:** 10 minutes **PRESSURE TIME:** 8 minutes **RELEASE METHOD:** Natural (10 minutes)

PREP INGREDIENTS

- 1 pound boneless, skinless chicken thighs, cut into 1-inch pieces
- 1 tablespoon minced fresh ginger
- 3 cloves garlic, minced
- 2 tablespoons canola oil
- ¼ cup packed brown sugar
- 1 tablespoon oyster sauce
- 2 tablespoons soy sauce

SERVING DAY INGREDIENTS

- 1 cup chicken stock
- 1 (16-ounce) package frozen broccoli
- 2 tablespoons cornstarch
- 3 tablespoons cold water
- 1 tablespoon sesame seeds (optional)

PREP DIRECTIONS

Combine the prep ingredients in a 1-gallon resealable freezer bag. Squeeze out the air, seal, label, and place in a round container to freeze into shape.

SERVING DAY DIRECTIONS

Add the stock and the contents of the package to the multi-cooker inner pot. Cook on high pressure for 8 minutes.

Let the pressure release naturally for 10 minutes, and then manually release any remaining pressure.

Set the pot to Sauté. Stir in the frozen broccoli and cook until heated through.

In a small bowl, mix together the cornstarch and water. Stir in the cornstarch mixture and cook until the sauce is thickened. If desired, sprinkle with the sesame seeds.

SESAME-ORANGE CHICKEN

Skip the takeout, and turn to your freezer to make this Chinese favorite in no time! Your family will love the bright orange flavor. You'll love how simple it is to whip up in your pressure cooker. Bonus: It smells delightful while it's cooking. Serve over rice.

SERVES: 4 **PREP TIME:** 15 minutes **PRESSURE TIME:** 8 minutes **RELEASE METHOD:** Natural (10 minutes)

PREP INGREDIENTS

- 1½ pounds boneless, skinless chicken thighs, cut into 1-inch pieces
- 3 cloves garlic, minced
- 1 tablespoon minced ginger
- ½ cup orange marmalade
- ¼ cup hoisin sauce
- 2 tablespoons soy sauce
- 1 tablespoon rice vinegar (or more as needed to balance sweetness)

SERVING DAY INGREDIENTS

- 1 cup chicken stock
- 2 tablespoons cornstarch
- 3 tablespoons cold water
- 2 green onions, thinly sliced
- 1 tablespoon sesame seeds

PREP DIRECTIONS

Combine the prep ingredients in a 1-gallon resealable freezer bag. Squeeze out the air, seal, label, and place in a round container to freeze into shape.

SERVING DAY DIRECTIONS

Add the stock and the contents of the package to the multi-cooker inner pot. Cook on high pressure for 8 minutes.

Let the pressure release naturally for 10 minutes, and then release any remaining pressure.

In a small bowl, stir together the cornstarch and water. Set the pot to Sauté, and stir in the cornstarch mixture until the sauce is slightly thickened. Stir in the green onions and sesame seeds.

CASHEW CHICKEN

This tender chicken in garlicky soy sauce with bright vegetables and crunchy cashews is just as delicious as takeout but much closer . . . waiting in your freezer. If you're really crunched for time, it's not essential to toast the cashews, although the roasted flavor is amazing. Serve over rice.

SERVES: 4   **PREP TIME:** 15 minutes   **PRESSURE TIME:** 8 minutes   **RELEASE METHOD:** Natural (10 minutes)

PREP INGREDIENTS

- 1½ pounds boneless, skinless chicken thighs, cut into 1-inch pieces
- 1 carrot, peeled and thinly sliced
- 1 rib celery, thinly sliced
- 1 green or red bell pepper, seeded and cut into 1-inch chunks
- 1 tablespoon minced ginger
- 3 cloves garlic, minced
- 2 tablespoons soy sauce
- 2 tablespoons dry sherry
- 1 tablespoon oyster sauce
  Salt to taste

SERVING DAY INGREDIENTS

- 1 cup chicken stock
- ⅓ cup cashews
- 2 cups frozen broccoli, thawed
- 2 tablespoons cornstarch
- 3 tablespoons cold water

PREP DIRECTIONS

Combine the prep ingredients in a 1-gallon resealable freezer bag. Squeeze out the air, seal, label, and place in a round container to freeze into shape.

SERVING DAY DIRECTIONS

Add the stock and the contents of the package to the multi-cooker inner pot. Cook on high pressure for 8 minutes.

Let the pressure release naturally for 10 minutes, and then manually release any remaining pressure. Add the broccoli florets and cook for a few minutes until slightly tender. Meanwhile, place the cashews in a dry skillet over medium heat. Toast, stirring occasionally, until lightly browned, 3 to 4 minutes. Set aside.

In a small bowl, stir together the cornstarch and water. Set the pot to Sauté, and stir in the reserved cashews and the cornstarch mixture. Cook, stirring, until the sauce is slightly thickened.

MEDITERRANEAN CHICKEN

With lots of flavor and very little prep, this chicken dinner is truly a winner. The delicious mix of garlic, herbs, wine, olives, and tomatoes will transform your dinner table into a Mediterranean café any night of the week. For extra zest, add just a pinch of crushed red pepper.

SERVES: 4   **PREP TIME:** 10 minutes   **PRESSURE TIME:** 10 minutes   **RELEASE METHOD:** Natural (10 minutes)

PREP INGREDIENTS

6   boneless, skinless chicken thighs, cut into 1½-inch pieces

1   cup canned diced tomatoes

2   tablespoons olive oil

3   cloves garlic, crushed

¼   teaspoon dried rosemary

½   teaspoon dried oregano

     Salt to taste

SERVING DAY INGREDIENTS

½   cup dry white wine

½   cup chicken stock

¼   cup coarsely chopped oil-cured olives

2   tablespoons chopped parsley

PREP DIRECTIONS

Combine the prep ingredients in a 1-gallon resealable freezer bag. Squeeze out the air, seal, label, and place in a round container to freeze into shape.

SERVING DAY DIRECTIONS

Add the wine, the chicken stock, and the contents of the package to the multi-cooker inner pot. Cook on high pressure for 10 minutes.

Let the pressure release naturally for 10 minutes, and then manually release any remaining pressure. Stir in the olives and chopped parsley.

CHICKEN CACCIATORE

With a rich and rustic sauce, chicken cacciatore is a classic one-dish dinner that often calls for an hour or more of simmering. This version puts your pressure cooker to work to take that process down to 15 minutes—without sacrificing depth of flavor. Make a side of pasta while it cooks, and you're all set.

SERVES: 4   **PREP TIME:** 15 minutes   **PRESSURE TIME:** 10 minutes   **RELEASE METHOD:** Natural (5 minutes)

PREP INGREDIENTS

- 2 pounds boneless, skinless chicken thighs, cut into 1½-inch pieces
- 1 onion, chopped
- 3 cloves garlic, minced
- 1 (14.5-ounce) can diced tomatoes, drained
- 2 tablespoons tomato paste
- 1 tablespoon Italian seasoning
  Salt to taste

SERVING DAY INGREDIENTS

- ½ cup dry red wine
- ½ cup chicken stock

PREP DIRECTIONS

Combine the prep ingredients in a 1-gallon resealable freezer bag. Squeeze out the air, seal, label, and place in a round container to freeze into shape.

SERVING DAY DIRECTIONS

Add the wine, the chicken stock, and the contents of the package to the multi-cooker inner pot. Cook on high pressure for 10 minutes.

Let the pressure release naturally for 5 minutes, and then manually release any remaining pressure.

CHICKEN PAPRIKASH

The star in this famous Hungarian recipe is paprika, but not just any paprika will do. Use a Hungarian-style sweet paprika that you'll find in a small tin in the spice aisle. It will give the dish a wonderfully bright orange color and amazing flavor. Serve over noodles.

SERVES: 4   **PREP TIME:** 15 minutes   **PRESSURE TIME:** 8 minutes   **RELEASE METHOD:** Natural (10 minutes)

PREP INGREDIENTS

2   pounds boneless, skinless chicken thighs, cut into 1½-inch pieces

1   onion, chopped

1   red bell pepper, seeded and sliced

1   plum tomato, seeded and chopped

2   tablespoons Hungarian sweet paprika

2   tablespoons tomato paste

Salt to taste

SERVING DAY INGREDIENTS

1   cup chicken stock

½   cup sour cream

PREP DIRECTIONS

Combine the prep ingredients in a 1-gallon resealable freezer bag. Squeeze out the air, seal, label, and place in a round container to freeze into shape.

SERVING DAY DIRECTIONS

Add the stock and the contents of the package to the multi-cooker inner pot. Cook on high pressure for 8 minutes.

Let the pressure release naturally for 10 minutes, and then manually release any remaining pressure. If you wish, turn the pot to Sauté and reduce the sauce to the desired consistency. Stir in the sour cream.

LEMON-GARLIC CHICKEN WITH SPINACH

The creamy sauce featured in this dinner is a dream! Wondering why so much garlic? A pressure cooker tends to mellow the flavor of garlic, so to give the dish a punch, stir in a teaspoon of raw minced garlic at the end. (You can always add more if you love garlic!) Serve over egg noodles or fettuccine.

SERVES: 4   **PREP TIME:** 10 minutes   **PRESSURE TIME:** 8 minutes   **RELEASE METHOD:** Natural (10 minutes)

PREP INGREDIENTS

- 2 pounds boneless, skinless chicken thighs, cut into 1½-inch pieces
- 5 cloves garlic, minced
  Several sprigs fresh thyme or 1 teaspoon dried thyme
  Zest of 1 lemon
- 1 tablespoon lemon juice
- ¼ cup white wine
  Salt and pepper to taste

SERVING DAY INGREDIENTS

- 1 cup chicken stock
- ½ cup heavy cream
- 2 tablespoons unsalted butter
- 1 teaspoon minced garlic
- 1 (5-ounce) bag baby spinach

PREP DIRECTIONS

Combine the prep ingredients in a 1-gallon resealable freezer bag. Squeeze out the air, seal, label, and place in a round container to freeze into shape.

SERVING DAY DIRECTIONS

Add the stock and the contents of the package to the multi-cooker inner pot. Cook on high pressure for 8 minutes.

Let the pressure release naturally for 10 minutes, and then manually release any remaining pressure.

Remove the thyme sprigs. If the sauce is too thin, transfer the chicken to a plate, turn the pot to Sauté, and simmer until the sauce reaches the desired consistency. Stir in the heavy cream, butter, minced garlic, and baby spinach until the spinach is just wilted.

CHICKEN WITH RED WINE SAUCE

This dish takes flavor inspiration from the French dish coq au vin but simplifies with boneless, skinless thighs versus a whole chicken. If you wish, you can add 8 ounces sliced mushrooms before you thicken the sauce. Just cook them a few extra minutes until tender. Serve with crusty bread or mashed potatoes.

SERVES: 4   **PREP TIME:** 15 minutes   **PRESSURE TIME:** 8 minutes   **RELEASE METHOD:** Natural

PREP INGREDIENTS

- 2 pounds boneless, skinless chicken thighs, cut into 2-inch pieces
- 4 ounces pancetta or ham steak, diced
- ½ pound baby carrots, halved
- 1 onion, chopped
- 2 cloves garlic, minced
- 1 cup dry red wine
- 3 sprigs fresh thyme or ½ teaspoon dried thyme
- 1 bay leaf (optional)
- Salt and pepper to taste

SERVING DAY INGREDIENTS

- 1 cup chicken stock
- 1 tablespoon cornstarch (optional)
- 2 tablespoons cold water (optional)
- 2 tablespoons unsalted butter
- 2 tablespoons chopped fresh parsley

PREP DIRECTIONS

Combine the prep ingredients in a 1-gallon resealable freezer bag. Squeeze out the air, seal, label, and place in a round container to freeze into shape.

SERVING DAY DIRECTIONS

Add the stock and the contents of the package to the multi-cooker inner pot. Cook on high pressure for 8 minutes.

Let the pressure release naturally. If the sauce is too thin, in a small bowl, stir together the cornstarch and water. Set the pot to Sauté, and stir in the cornstarch mixture until the sauce is slightly thickened. Stir in the butter and fresh parsley. Remove the bay leaf and thyme sprigs before serving.

CREAMY SUN-DRIED TOMATO CHICKEN

Make this dish once and your family will request it again and again! It's a good thing that this recipe is so simple to make with the Fix 'n' Freeze method. For a flavor twist, replace the heavy cream with full-fat coconut milk. Serve over pasta or quinoa.

SERVES: 4 **PREP TIME:** 10 minutes **PRESSURE TIME:** 8 minutes **RELEASE METHOD:** Natural (10 minutes)

PREP INGREDIENTS

- 2 pounds boneless, skinless chicken thighs
- ½ cup chopped sun-dried tomatoes in oil
- 2 cloves garlic, minced
- 1 tablespoon red wine vinegar
- 2 teaspoons Italian seasoning
  Salt to taste

SERVING DAY INGREDIENTS

- 1 cup chicken stock
- ½ cup grated Parmesan cheese
- ½ cup heavy cream
- ½ cup thinly sliced basil leaves

PREP DIRECTIONS

Combine the prep ingredients in a 1-gallon resealable freezer bag. Squeeze out the air, seal, label, and place in a round container to freeze into shape.

SERVING DAY DIRECTIONS

Add the stock and the contents of the package to the multi-cooker inner pot. Cook on high pressure for 8 minutes.

Let the pressure release naturally for 10 minutes, and then manually release any remaining pressure. Stir in the Parmesan, heavy cream, and basil leaves.

LEMON CHICKEN WITH FENNEL

No more boring chicken dinners! Fennel has a mild anise flavor that pairs well with lemon in your kitchen. Using chicken thighs guarantees moist, flavorful meat. Bringing them all together in your pressure cooker is dinner magic in less than 20 minutes.

SERVES: 4 **PREP TIME:** 15 minutes **PRESSURE TIME:** 8 minutes **RELEASE METHOD:** Natural (10 minutes)

PREP INGREDIENTS

- 2 pounds boneless, skinless chicken thighs, cut into 1½-inch pieces
- 1 large bulb fennel, thinly sliced
- 3 cloves garlic, minced
- 1 tablespoon lemon juice
- Salt and pepper to taste

SERVING DAY INGREDIENTS

- 1 cup chicken stock
- 1 tablespoon cornstarch (optional)
- 2 tablespoons cold water (optional)
- 2 tablespoons unsalted butter
- Lemon wedges, for serving

PREP DIRECTIONS

Combine the prep ingredients in a 1-gallon resealable freezer bag. Squeeze out the air, seal, label, and place in a round container to freeze into shape.

SERVING DAY DIRECTIONS

Add the stock and the contents of the package to the multi-cooker inner pot. Cook on high pressure for 8 minutes.

Let the pressure release naturally for 10 minutes, and then manually release any remaining pressure.

If the sauce is too thin, in a small bowl stir together the cornstarch and water. Set the pot to Sauté, and stir in the cornstarch mixture until the sauce is slightly thickened. Stir in the butter until melted. Serve with lemon wedges.

BALSAMIC-ROSEMARY CHICKEN

So classic, so easy—this is the chicken recipe everyone needs! It fits any occasion, from a weeknight family dinner to entertaining. If you ever have leftovers (chances are slim), they're delicious tossed over a green salad or cold pasta or grain salad.

SERVES: 4   **PREP TIME:** 15 minutes   **PRESSURE TIME:** 8 minutes   **RELEASE METHOD:** Natural

PREP INGREDIENTS

- 2 pounds boneless, skinless chicken thighs, cut into 2-inch pieces
- 2 tablespoons balsamic vinegar
- 2 tablespoons olive oil
- 2 teaspoons chopped fresh rosemary
- 3 cloves garlic, minced
  Zest of 1 lemon
  Salt and pepper to taste

SERVING DAY INGREDIENTS

- 1 cup chicken stock
  Lemon wedges, for serving

PREP DIRECTIONS

Combine the prep ingredients in a 1-gallon resealable freezer bag. Squeeze out the air, seal, label, and place in a round container to freeze into shape.

SERVING DAY DIRECTIONS

Add the stock and the contents of the package to the multi-cooker inner pot. Cook on high pressure for 8 minutes.

Let the pressure release naturally. Serve with lemon wedges.

POTSTICKER TURKEY MEATBALLS

Get right to all the meat you love in dumplings or pot stickers! Preparing the meat without the wrappers speeds the process and lowers the carb count, if you're watching. Using ground turkey also gives the meatballs a lighter take that's just as delicious as beef or pork.

SERVES: 4   **PREP TIME:** 20 minutes   **PRESSURE TIME:** 7 minutes   **RELEASE METHOD:** Natural (10 minutes)

PREP INGREDIENTS

- 1½ pounds ground turkey
- 2 cloves garlic, minced
- 2 teaspoons minced fresh ginger
- 3 tablespoons soy sauce
- 1 tablespoon toasted sesame oil
- 1 tablespoon dry sherry
- 1 tablespoon hoisin or oyster sauce
- ¼ cup panko breadcrumbs
- ¼ cup chopped fresh cilantro (optional)
- 3 green onions, minced
- ¼ teaspoon salt
- ½ teaspoon white pepper

SERVING DAY INGREDIENTS

- 1½ cups plus 2 tablespoons water, divided
- ½ cup soy sauce
- 2 tablespoons rice vinegar
- 1 teaspoon toasted sesame oil

PREP DIRECTIONS

In a large bowl, mix together the prep ingredients. Roll the mixture into 1½-inch balls, place on a parchment paper–lined baking sheet, and freeze. Once the meatballs are completely frozen, transfer them to a 1-gallon resealable freezer bag. Squeeze out the air, seal, label, and place in a round container to freeze into shape.

SERVING DAY DIRECTIONS

Add 1½ cups of the water and the trivet to the multi-cooker inner pot. Place a steamer basket on top of the trivet and add the meatballs. Cook on high pressure for 7 minutes.

Let the pressure release naturally for 10 minutes, and then manually release any remaining pressure. For the dipping sauce, mix together the soy sauce, vinegar, sesame oil, and remaining 2 tablespoons water in a small bowl.

BEEF
& PORK

CLASSIC POT ROAST

A trusty pot roast recipe can be your best culinary friend, especially on a cold day. With the Fix 'n' Freeze method, you no longer need to wait until the weekend for that roast. Just 20 minutes in your pressure cooker is all your roast needs to cook up tenderly and deliciously.

SERVES: 4 to 6   **PREP TIME:** 15 minutes   **PRESSURE TIME:** 20 minutes   **RELEASE METHOD:** Natural

PREP INGREDIENTS

- 2 pounds chuck roast, cut into 2-inch pieces
- 2 large onions, cut into wedges
- 2 carrots, peeled and sliced into 2-inch pieces
- 2 ribs celery, cut into 2-inch pieces
- 1 bay leaf
- 2 teaspoons salt
- 1 teaspoon black pepper
- 2 sprigs fresh rosemary
- 2 sprigs fresh thyme

SERVING DAY INGREDIENTS

- ½ cup dry red wine
- ½ cup chicken stock
- 2 tablespoons cornstarch
- 3 tablespoons cold water

PREP DIRECTIONS

Combine the prep ingredients in a 1-gallon resealable freezer bag. Squeeze out the air, seal, label, and place in a round container to freeze into shape.

SERVING DAY DIRECTIONS

Add the red wine and the chicken stock (or use all stock) and the contents of the package to the multi-cooker inner pot. Cook on high pressure for 20 minutes.

Let the pressure release naturally. Remove and discard the bay leaf and herb sprigs. Remove the meat and vegetables to a serving dish and tent with foil.

In a small bowl, mix together the cornstarch and water. Set the pot to Sauté, and stir in the cornstarch mixture until the sauce is slightly thickened. Spoon the sauce over the meat and vegetables.

ITALIAN POT ROAST

Fragrant herbs, tomatoes, red wine, tangy pepperoncini, and cubes of beef come together in your pressure cooker to create a perfectly tender pot roast that's full of flavor but doesn't require hours of cooking time. Try it served over polenta.

SERVES: 4 to 6   **PREP TIME:** 15 minutes   **PRESSURE TIME:** 20 minutes   **RELEASE METHOD:** Natural

PREP INGREDIENTS

- 2 pounds chuck roast, cut into 2-inch cubes
- 1 onion, chopped
- 3 cloves garlic, minced
- 1 carrot, peeled and chopped
- 1 rib celery, chopped
- 4 jarred pepperoncini, sliced (optional)
- 1 tablespoon Italian seasoning
- 2 tablespoons tomato paste
- 1 (14.5-ounce) can crushed tomatoes
- Salt and pepper to taste

SERVING DAY INGREDIENTS

- ½ cup dry red wine
- ½ cup chicken stock

PREP DIRECTIONS

Combine the prep ingredients in a 1-gallon resealable freezer bag. Squeeze out the air, seal, label, and place in a round container to freeze into shape.

SERVING DAY DIRECTIONS

Add the wine, the stock, and the contents of the package to the multi-cooker inner pot. Cook on high pressure for 20 minutes, and then let the pressure release naturally.

TUSCAN BEEF WITH RED WINE

Although garlic (and more garlic!) is the featured seasoning here, pancetta—a cured unsmoked Italian bacon—also brings rich flavor to this hearty dish. If you have trouble finding pancetta, cubes of ham steak work nicely as a substitute.

SERVES: 4   **PREP TIME:** 15 minutes   **PRESSURE TIME:** 20 minutes   **RELEASE METHOD:** Natural

PREP INGREDIENTS

- 2   pounds chuck roast, cut into 1½-inch pieces
- 4   ounces pancetta, finely diced
- 1   onion, chopped
- 4   cloves garlic, chopped
- 2   carrots, chopped
- 2   sprigs thyme
     Salt and pepper to taste

SERVING DAY INGREDIENTS

- ½   cup dry red wine
- ½   cup beef or chicken stock
- 1   tablespoon minced garlic
- 2   tablespoons cornstarch
- 3   tablespoons cold water

PREP DIRECTIONS

Combine the prep ingredients in a 1-gallon resealable freezer bag. Squeeze out the air, seal, label, and place in a round container to freeze into shape.

SERVING DAY DIRECTIONS

Add the wine, the stock, and the contents of the package to the multi-cooker inner pot. Cook on high pressure for 20 minutes.

Let the pressure release naturally. Remove the thyme sprigs. Stir in the minced garlic.

In a small bowl, mix together the cornstarch and water. Set the pot to Sauté, and stir in the cornstarch mixture until the sauce is slightly thickened.

BEEF GOULASH

Goulash is simply a stew of beef and vegetables seasoned with paprika that originated in Hungary. For the best flavor, use a Hungarian-style paprika; it's a worthy, hardworking addition to your spice collection if you don't have it on hand. Serve over buttered noodles or rice with dollops of sour cream.

SERVES: 4   **PREP TIME:** 10 minutes   **PRESSURE TIME:** 20 minutes   **RELEASE METHOD:** Natural

PREP INGREDIENTS

- 2 pounds chuck roast, cut into 1-inch cubes
- 2 onions, coarsely chopped
- 2 green bell peppers, seeded and chopped
  Salt and pepper to taste
- 2 tablespoons Hungarian sweet paprika

SERVING DAY INGREDIENTS

- 1 cup beef stock
- 2 tablespoons unsalted butter

PREP DIRECTIONS

Combine the prep ingredients in a 1-gallon resealable freezer bag. Squeeze out the air, seal, label, and place in a round container to freeze into shape.

SERVING DAY DIRECTIONS

Add the stock and the contents of the package to the multi-cooker inner pot. Cook on high pressure for 20 minutes, and then let the pressure release naturally. Stir in the butter until melted.

PEPPER STEAK

This popular Chinese-American dish is both flavorful with thinly sliced and seasoned flank steak and colorful with red and green bell peppers. You can customize vegetables to what you enjoy or have on hand—try carrots, any color of bell pepper, asparagus, broccoli, or even water chestnuts for some new ideas. Serve over rice.

SERVES: 4   **PREP TIME:** 15 minutes   **PRESSURE TIME:** 10 minutes   **RELEASE METHOD:** Natural (10 minutes)

PREP INGREDIENTS

- 1 pound flank steak, thinly sliced
- 1 red bell pepper, seeded and sliced
- 1 green bell pepper, seeded and sliced
- 1 onion, halved and thinly sliced
- 3 cloves garlic, minced
- 1 teaspoon ground ginger
  Salt to taste
- 1 teaspoon black pepper
- 2 tablespoons dry sherry
- 2 tablespoons hoisin sauce
- 1 tablespoon soy sauce

SERVING DAY INGREDIENTS

- 1 cup chicken or beef stock
- 2 tablespoons cornstarch
- 3 tablespoons cold water
- 1 teaspoon toasted sesame oil

PREP DIRECTIONS

Combine the prep ingredients in a 1-gallon resealable freezer bag. Squeeze out the air, seal, label, and place in a round container to freeze into shape.

SERVING DAY DIRECTIONS

Add the stock and the contents of the package to the multi-cooker inner pot. Cook on high pressure for 10 minutes.

Let the pressure release naturally for 10 minutes, and then manually release any remaining pressure.

In a small bowl, mix together the cornstarch and water. Set the pot to Sauté, and stir in the cornstarch mixture until the sauce is slightly thickened. Stir in the sesame oil.

BEEF AND BROCCOLI

The next time you're thinking of takeout, simply take the prepped ingredients for this restaurant-quality dish out of your freezer. Thinly sliced seasoned beef and crisp-tender broccoli will emerge from your pressure cooker in 20 minutes. Serve over rice.

SERVES: 4 to 6   **PREP TIME:** 15 minutes   **PRESSURE TIME:** 10 minutes   **RELEASE METHOD:** Natural (10 minutes)

PREP INGREDIENTS

- 1½ pounds flank steak, thinly sliced into ½-inch by 2-inch pieces
- 1 large onion, thinly sliced
- 3 cloves garlic, minced
- 1 tablespoon minced ginger
  Salt and pepper to taste
- 2 tablespoons soy sauce
- 2 tablespoons oyster sauce
- 1 tablespoon dry sherry

SERVING DAY INGREDIENTS

- 1 cup chicken stock
- 1 pound broccoli florets (fresh or frozen)
- 2 tablespoons cornstarch
- 3 tablespoons cold water
- 1 teaspoon sesame oil (optional)

PREP DIRECTIONS

Combine the prep ingredients in a 1-gallon resealable freezer bag. Squeeze out the air, seal, label, and place in a round container to freeze into shape.

SERVING DAY DIRECTIONS

Add the stock and the contents of the package to the multi-cooker inner pot. Cook on high pressure for 10 minutes.

Let the pressure release naturally for 10 minutes, and then manually release any remaining pressure. Add the broccoli florets and cook for a few minutes until slightly tender.

In a small bowl, mix together the cornstarch and water. Set the pot to Sauté, and stir in the cornstarch mixture until the sauce is slightly thickened. Add the sesame oil, if desired.

SWISS STEAK

Traditional Swiss steak calls for hours of cooking to get fall-apart meat. But pressure cooking in a simple tomato sauce transforms an inexpensive cut of steak into a tender and amazing dish in much less time! Serve it over mashed potatoes, rice, or egg noodles for comfort food in a flash.

SERVES: 4   **PREP TIME:** 15 minutes   **PRESSURE TIME:** 20 minutes   **RELEASE METHOD:** Natural (10 minutes)

PREP INGREDIENTS

- 2 pounds blade steak, cut into 2-inch pieces
- 1 (0.7-ounce) packet Italian dressing mix
- 1 onion, chopped
- 3 cloves garlic, minced
- 1 (14.5-ounce) can diced tomatoes
- 2 tablespoons tomato paste
- 1 tablespoon soy sauce
- 1 tablespoon red wine vinegar
- ½ teaspoon black pepper

SERVING DAY INGREDIENTS

- 1 cup chicken or beef stock
  Chopped fresh parsley, for garnish (optional)

PREP DIRECTIONS

Combine the prep ingredients in a 1-gallon resealable freezer bag. Squeeze out the air, seal, label, and place in a round container to freeze into shape.

SERVING DAY DIRECTIONS

Add the stock and the contents of the package to the multi-cooker inner pot. Cook on high pressure for 20 minutes.

Let the pressure release naturally for 10 minutes, and then manually release any remaining pressure. Sprinkle with chopped fresh parsley, if desired.

KOREAN-STYLE SHORT RIBS

With a little prep, these ribs are ready to become your amazing dinner in 30 minutes. If you like charred flavor, add one simple step at the end of the directions: place the ribs on a rack set inside a rimmed baking sheet and broil until lightly charred on both sides, about 1 minute per side. Serve over rice.

SERVES: 4   **PREP TIME:** 15 minutes   **PRESSURE TIME:** 20 minutes   **RELEASE METHOD:** Natural (10 minutes)

PREP INGREDIENTS

- 2 pounds boneless beef short ribs, cut into 1½-inch pieces
- 1 onion, chopped
- 2 carrots, peeled and sliced
- 4 cloves garlic, minced
- 1 tablespoon minced ginger
- ½ cup soy sauce

SERVING DAY INGREDIENTS

- 1 cup beef stock
- 1 tablespoon toasted sesame oil
- 2 teaspoons sesame seeds (optional)

PREP DIRECTIONS

Combine the prep ingredients in a 1-gallon resealable freezer bag. Squeeze out the air, seal, label, and place in a round container to freeze into shape.

SERVING DAY DIRECTIONS

Add the stock and the contents of the package to the multi-cooker inner pot. Cook on high pressure for 20 minutes.

Let the pressure release naturally for 10 minutes, and then manually release any remaining pressure. Stir in the sesame oil and sprinkle with the sesame seeds, if using.

SMOTHERED SHORT RIBS

Five simple ingredients work with pressure cooking to give you flavorful, fall-apart tender short ribs. Smothered in onions, beer, and French onion soup, these ribs are perfection served over mashed potatoes with a generous helping of the gravy.

SERVES: 4 to 6   **PREP TIME:** 10 minutes   **PRESSURE TIME:** 20 minutes   **RELEASE METHOD:** Natural (10 minutes)

PREP INGREDIENTS

2   pounds boneless beef short ribs, cut into 1-inch pieces
    Salt and pepper to taste

2   onions, thinly sliced

1   (10.5-ounce) can French onion soup

1   tablespoon Worcestershire sauce

SERVING DAY INGREDIENTS

1   cup beer

PREP DIRECTIONS

Season the beef with salt and pepper. Add the beef and the remaining prep ingredients to a 1-gallon resealable freezer bag. Squeeze out the air, seal, label, and place in a round container to freeze into shape.

SERVING DAY DIRECTIONS

Add the beer and the contents of the package to the multi-cooker inner pot. Cook on high pressure for 20 minutes.

Let the pressure release naturally for 10 minutes, and then manually release any remaining pressure. Turn the pot to Sauté and simmer the sauce for a few minutes to thicken.

FAVORITE ITALIAN MEATBALLS

You can serve homemade meatballs any time! All you need are the prep ingredients waiting in your freezer and your pressure cooker. Company drops in? Kids' activities run late? Count down just 16 minutes to classic Italian meatballs for dinner.

SERVES: 4 to 6   **PREP TIME:** 20 minutes   **PRESSURE TIME:** 6 minutes   **RELEASE METHOD:** Natural (10 minutes)

PREP INGREDIENTS

- 1½ pounds ground beef
- 2 tablespoons minced onion
- 2 cloves garlic, minced
- 1 large egg, beaten
- ½ cup breadcrumbs
- ¼ cup minced fresh parsley
- 1 teaspoon salt
- ¼ teaspoon ground pepper

SERVING DAY INGREDIENTS

- 1½ cups water
- 1 (25-ounce) jar tomato sauce

PREP DIRECTIONS

In a large bowl, mix together all of the prep ingredients. Roll the mixture into 1½-inch balls, place on a parchment paper–lined baking sheet, and freeze.

Once the meatballs are completely frozen, transfer them to a 1-gallon resealable freezer bag. Squeeze out the air, seal, label, and place in a round container to freeze into shape.

SERVING DAY DIRECTIONS

Add the water, the tomato sauce, and the meatballs to the multi-cooker inner pot. Cook on high pressure for 6 minutes.

Let the pressure release naturally for 10 minutes, and then manually release any remaining pressure.

SALISBURY STEAK MEATBALLS

Try this new twist on traditional Salisbury steak! Its amazing throwback flavor meets fun, easy preparation and serving with store-bought meatballs and your pressure cooker. Topped with creamy mushroom gravy, the meatballs pair really well with mashed potatoes or buttered noodles. For a healthier take, toss over mashed cauliflower.

SERVES: 4   **PREP TIME:** 10 minutes   **PRESSURE TIME:** 8 minutes   **RELEASE METHOD:** Natural (10 minutes)

PREP INGREDIENTS

- 1 (2-pound) bag fully cooked frozen meatballs
- 1 large onion, thinly sliced
- ½ cup dry white wine
- 1 tablespoon tomato paste
- ½ teaspoon dried thyme
- 1 (0.87-ounce) package brown gravy mix

SERVING DAY INGREDIENTS

- 1 cup water
- 8 ounces mushrooms, sliced (optional)
- 2 tablespoons chopped fresh parsley
- 2 tablespoons cornstarch (optional)
- 3 tablespoons cold water (optional)

PREP DIRECTIONS

Combine the prep ingredients in a 1-gallon resealable freezer bag. Squeeze out the air, seal, label, and place in a round container to freeze into shape.

SERVING DAY DIRECTIONS

Add the water and the contents of the package to the multi-cooker inner pot. Cook on high pressure for 8 minutes.

Let the pressure release naturally for 10 minutes, and then manually release any remaining pressure. Add the mushrooms, if desired, and the parsley. Set the pot to Sauté and cook until the mushrooms are slightly tender.

If the sauce is too thin, in a small bowl, stir together the cornstarch and water. With the pot on Sauté, stir in the cornstarch mixture until the sauce is slightly thickened.

PICADILLO

Although most classic picadillo recipes include ground beef, onion, tomato, olives, and raisins, this traditional Latin American dish is very much like chili in that there are many variations. It's easy to master this recipe in a pressure cooker and then adapt it to your family's liking. If you somehow happen to have leftovers, picadillo is tasty in empanadas and quesadillas.

SERVES: 4 to 6   **PREP TIME:** 15 minutes   **PRESSURE TIME:** 7 minutes   **RELEASE METHOD:** Natural (5 minutes)

PREP INGREDIENTS

1   pound ground beef, browned, drained, and cooled

1   pound fresh chorizo sausage, casing removed, browned, drained, and cooled

1   onion, chopped

3   cloves garlic, minced

1   cup canned diced tomatoes, drained

1   tablespoon vinegar

½   cup coarsely chopped pimento-stuffed green olives or black olives

⅓   cup raisins (optional)

½   teaspoon dried oregano

½   teaspoon ground cumin

    Salt and pepper to taste

SERVING DAY INGREDIENTS

1   cup chicken or beef stock

2   tablespoons cornstarch (optional)

3   tablespoons cold water (optional)

PREP DIRECTIONS

Combine the prep ingredients in a 1-gallon resealable freezer bag. Squeeze out the air, seal, label, and place in a round container to freeze into shape.

SERVING DAY DIRECTIONS

Add the stock and the contents of the package to the multi-cooker inner pot. Cook on high pressure for 7 minutes.

Let the pressure release naturally for 5 minutes, and then manually release the pressure.

If the sauce is too thin, in a small bowl, stir together the cornstarch and water. Set the pot to Sauté, and stir in the cornstarch mixture until the sauce is slightly thickened.

BEEF STROGANOFF

Swapping in ground meat makes this family favorite even easier and more budget friendly to prepare. It's a perfect comfort-food dish when served over egg noodles. While the pressure releases from the pot, cook up the noodles. Then pour on the rich, creamy beef!

SERVES: 4   **PREP TIME:** 20 minutes   **PRESSURE TIME:** 8 minutes   **RELEASE METHOD:** Natural (10 minutes)

PREP INGREDIENTS

2   tablespoons olive oil, divided

1½ pounds ground beef

1   pound mushrooms, sliced

1   large onion, chopped

2   cloves garlic, minced

2   tablespoons tomato paste

½   teaspoon ground thyme
    Salt and pepper to taste

1   tablespoon Worcestershire sauce

SERVING DAY INGREDIENTS

½   cup beef stock

½   cup dry red wine

1   (8-ounce) container sour cream

2   tablespoons chopped fresh parsley
    (optional)

PREP DIRECTIONS

Heat 1 tablespoon of the oil in a large skillet over medium heat. Add the beef and cook, breaking up large chunks with a wooden spoon. Drain the excess fat and transfer to a plate to cool. In the same pan, increase the heat to medium-high, add the remaining 1 tablespoon olive oil and the mushrooms, and cook, stirring occasionally, until golden brown. Set aside to cool. (You could use the Sauté setting in the multi-cooker, but it will be easier to cook the mushrooms in the skillet so that there's a larger surface area for them to brown.)

Add the cooled meat and mushrooms, along with the remaining prep ingredients, to a 1-gallon resealable freezer bag. Squeeze out the air, seal, label, and place in a round container to freeze into shape.

SERVING DAY DIRECTIONS

Add the stock, the red wine, and the contents of the package to the multi-cooker inner pot. Cook on high pressure for 8 minutes.

Let the pressure release naturally for 10 minutes, and then manually release any remaining pressure. Stir in the sour cream and parsley (if desired).

CARIBBEAN-STYLE PORK

Wake up any dinner with this pork dish seasoned with garlic, ginger, allspice, and thyme. To create a simple but satisfying one-bowl meal, serve over rice with black beans or mango salsa. Set out plantain chips for even more taste of the topics.

SERVES: 4   **PREP TIME:** 15 minutes   **PRESSURE TIME:** 15 minutes   **RELEASE METHOD:** Natural

PREP INGREDIENTS

- 2   pounds pork shoulder or butt, cut into 1-inch cubes
- 1   onion, chopped
- 3   cloves garlic, chopped
- 1   teaspoon ground ginger
- 1   teaspoon ground allspice
- 1   teaspoon ground thyme
- 1   teaspoon salt
- ½   cup orange juice

SERVING DAY INGREDIENTS

- 1   cup chicken or beef stock

PREP DIRECTIONS

Combine the prep ingredients in a 1-gallon resealable freezer bag. Squeeze out the air, seal, label, and place in a round container to freeze into shape.

SERVING DAY DIRECTIONS

Add the stock and the contents of the package to the multi-cooker inner pot. Cook on high pressure for 15 minutes.

Let the pressure release naturally. The pork should be fork-tender. Once cool enough to handle, shred the pork with two forks.

BRAISED PORK WITH CREAMY MUSTARD SAUCE

A French-inspired dinner doesn't need to be fussy to prepare. This tender pork dish goes from freezer to multi-cooker to table in 20 minutes. Complete the meal with a simple green salad and crusty bread for a dinner that tastes gourmet but won't cost you a lot of time or money.

SERVES: 4   **PREP TIME:** 10 minutes   **PRESSURE TIME:** 15 minutes   **RELEASE METHOD:** Natural

PREP INGREDIENTS

- 2 pounds pork shoulder, cut into 1-inch cubes
- 2 shallots, chopped
- 2 tablespoon grainy mustard
- 2 teaspoons Dijon mustard
- Salt and pepper to taste

SERVING DAY INGREDIENTS

- 1 cup chicken or beef stock
- 2 tablespoons cornstarch
- 3 tablespoons cold water
- ½ cup sour cream

PREP DIRECTIONS

Combine the prep ingredients in a 1-gallon resealable freezer bag. Squeeze out the air, seal, label, and place in a round container to freeze into shape.

SERVING DAY DIRECTIONS

Add the stock and the contents of the package to the multi-cooker inner pot. Cook on high pressure for 15 minutes.

Let the pressure release naturally. The pork should be fork-tender.

In a small bowl, stir together the cornstarch and water. Set the pot to Sauté, and stir in the cornstarch mixture until the sauce is slightly thickened. Stir in the sour cream.

CRANBERRY APPLE PORK LOIN

The aroma of fall smells so delicious coming from your pressure cooker! In just 30 minutes, you can serve a delicious combination of sweet and savory that works equally well for feeding your family any weeknight and entertaining guests. When selecting the pork, be sure to choose pork loin, not the small tenderloin.

SERVES: 4   **PREP TIME:** 15 minutes   **PRESSURE TIME:** 20 minutes   **RELEASE METHOD:** Natural (10 minutes)

PREP INGREDIENTS

- 2 pounds pork loin, cut into 1-inch cubes
- 3 cups cubed butternut squash
- ½ onion, chopped
- ⅓ cup dried cranberries
- ½ teaspoon dried sage
- ¼ teaspoon dried rosemary
  Salt and pepper to taste

SERVING DAY INGREDIENTS

- 1 cup apple cider
- 2 tablespoons cornstarch (optional)
- 2 tablespoons cold water (optional)
- 2 tablespoons unsalted butter

PREP DIRECTIONS

Combine the prep ingredients in a 1-gallon resealable freezer bag. Squeeze out the air, seal, label, and place in a round container to freeze into shape.

SERVING DAY DIRECTIONS

Add the apple cider and the contents of the package to the multi-cooker inner pot. Cook on high pressure for 20 minutes.

Let the pressure release naturally for 10 minutes, and then manually release any remaining pressure.

If the sauce is too thin, in a small bowl, mix together the cornstarch and water. Set the pot to Sauté, and stir in the cornstarch mixture until the sauce is slightly thickened. Stir in the butter until melted.

MAPLE PORK WITH SAUERKRAUT AND APPLES

Maple syrup is the perfect complement to pork flavored with sauerkraut and apples. The sweetest news: it will taste like you spent hours in the kitchen making dinner. In fact, this complete home-style meal is ready to enjoy in 30 minutes when you use the Fix 'n' Freeze method.

SERVES: 4 to 6   **PREP TIME:** 15 minutes   **PRESSURE TIME:** 20 minutes   **RELEASE METHOD:** Natural (10 minutes)

PREP INGREDIENTS

2   pounds pork loin or pork shoulder, cut into 1-inch pieces

1   apple, peeled and diced

1   onion, chopped

3   tablespoons maple syrup

Salt and pepper to taste

SERVING DAY INGREDIENTS

1   cup chicken stock

1   (14.5-ounce) container sauerkraut

2   tablespoons unsalted butter

Salt and pepper to taste

PREP DIRECTIONS

Combine the prep ingredients in a 1-gallon resealable freezer bag. Squeeze out the air, seal, label, and place in a round container to freeze into shape.

SERVING DAY DIRECTIONS

Add the stock and the contents of the package to the multi-cooker inner pot. Cook on high pressure for 20 minutes.

Let the pressure release naturally for 10 minutes, and then manually release any remaining pressure. Stir in the sauerkraut and butter until melted. Season to taste with salt and pepper.

FISH & SEAFOOD

GREEK-STYLE COD

Cod is a popular fish dinner because it's so budget friendly. But you don't need to sacrifice flavor to save money. Giving this simple fish just a few seasoning touches can transform its mild taste into full Mediterranean flavor that cooks up moist in minutes with your multi-cooker.

SERVES: 4   **PREP TIME:** 5 minutes   **PRESSURE TIME:** 2 minutes   **RELEASE METHOD:** Manual

PREP INGREDIENTS

- 4   (5- to 6-ounce) fillets fresh cod
  Salt and pepper to taste
- 2   teaspoons chopped fresh oregano or ½ teaspoon dried oregano
- 4   tablespoons chopped sun-dried tomatoes in oil
- 4   tablespoons sliced pitted kalamata olives
- 4   teaspoons extra-virgin olive oil

SERVING DAY INGREDIENTS

- 1   cup water
  Lemon wedges, for serving (optional)

PREP DIRECTIONS

Season each fillet with salt, pepper, and oregano. Top each fillet with 1 tablespoon sun-dried tomatoes and 1 tablespoon kalamata olives. Drizzle each with 1 teaspoon olive oil. Place each fillet on a parchment paper–lined sheet of aluminum foil. Wrap individually and place in a 1-gallon resealable freezer bag. Squeeze out the air, seal, label, and freeze.

SERVING DAY DIRECTIONS

Add the water and the trivet to the bottom of the multi-cooker. Place a piece of foil on top of the trivet to catch any drippings. Unwrap the fish and place the fillets on top of the trivet in a single layer (as flat as possible). Cook on low pressure for 2 minutes.

Manually release the pressure. Check for doneness. If desired, serve with lemon wedges.

LEMON-DILL COD

Lemon and dill is a classic flavor combination that works well for many types of fish. This recipe calls for cod, but you can easily swap in another thick white fish of your choice. While the multi-cooker isn't always the best place to cook something delicate like fish, frozen fish is a smart choice; it's much less likely to be overcooked.

SERVES: 4   **PREP TIME:** 5 minutes   **PRESSURE TIME:** 2 minutes   **RELEASE METHOD:** Manual

PREP INGREDIENTS

4   (5- to 6-ounce) fillets fresh cod
Salt and pepper to taste

2   tablespoons minced fresh dill fronds

4   tablespoons unsalted butter, sliced

4   thin slices lemon

SERVING DAY INGREDIENTS

1   cup water

PREP DIRECTIONS

Season each fillet with salt and pepper. Top each fillet with ½ tablespoon dill, 1 tablespoon butter, and 1 slice lemon. Place each fillet on a parchment paper–lined sheet of aluminum foil. Wrap individually and place in a 1-gallon resealable freezer bag. Squeeze out the air, seal, label, and freeze.

SERVING DAY DIRECTIONS

Add the water and the trivet to the bottom of the multi-cooker. Place a piece of foil on top of the trivet to catch any drippings. Unwrap the fish and place the fillets on top of the trivet in a single layer (as flat as possible). Cook on low pressure for 2 minutes.

Manually release the pressure. Check for doneness.

PESTO SALMON

This multi-cooker dish should be called presto salmon, because it comes together in a flash and with barely any real prep. All you need are the salmon and prepared pesto, and you're set for a gourmet dinner with no fuss but big flavor. A squeeze of fresh lemon is the perfect finishing touch.

SERVES: 4   **PREP TIME:** 5 minutes   **PRESSURE TIME:** 2 minutes   **RELEASE METHOD:** Manual

PREP INGREDIENTS

4   (5- to 6-ounce) fresh salmon fillets, preferably wild-caught

¼   to ⅓ cup homemade or store-bought pesto

SERVING DAY INGREDIENTS

1   cup water

Lemon wedges, for serving

PREP DIRECTIONS

Coat the salmon fillets with 1 tablespoon or so of the pesto. Place each fillet on a parchment paper–lined sheet of aluminum foil. Wrap each piece individually and place in a 1-gallon resealable freezer bag. Squeeze out the air, seal, label, and freeze.

SERVING DAY DIRECTIONS

Add the water and the trivet to the bottom of the multi-cooker. Place a piece of foil on top of the trivet to catch any drippings. Unwrap the fish and place the fillets on top of the trivet in a single layer (as flat as possible). Cook on low pressure for 2 minutes.

Manually release the pressure. Check for doneness. Spoon any extra pesto on top of the fish and serve with lemon wedges.

ANDOUILLE AND SHRIMP JAMBALAYA

Traditional jambalaya may call for an hour of cooking time! But you don't need to make that kind of time investment to add a Creole taste celebration to your dinner table when you pair easy freezer prep with 12 minutes in your multi-cooker. To keep the meal freezer friendly, the rice is cooked up separately on serving day.

SERVES: 4 to 6   **PREP TIME:** 10 minutes   **PRESSURE TIME:** 7 minutes   **RELEASE METHOD:** Natural (5 minutes)

PREP INGREDIENTS

- 1 pound cooked andouille sausage, cut into 1-inch-thick slices
- 1 onion, chopped
- 1 green bell pepper, seeded and chopped
- 2 teaspoons Cajun seasoning
- 1 (8-ounce) can tomato sauce
- 1 tablespoon Worcestershire or soy sauce

  Salt and pepper to taste

SERVING DAY INGREDIENTS

- 1 cup chicken stock
- 1 pound fresh shrimp, peeled and deveined
- 2 cups rice, cooked according to package directions

PREP DIRECTIONS

Combine the prep ingredients in a 1-gallon resealable freezer bag. Squeeze out the air, seal, label, and place in a round container to freeze into shape.

SERVING DAY DIRECTIONS

Add the stock and the contents of the package to the multi-cooker inner pot. Cook on high pressure for 7 minutes.

Let the pressure release naturally for 5 minutes, and then manually release any remaining pressure.

Stir in the shrimp, replace the lid on the pot but do not lock it, and let the shrimp cook in the residual heat, about 4 minutes. When cooked through, serve over the rice, or stir the rice into the pot and serve from there.

HERB-CRUSTED SALMON

Salmon is so good for you! If you're looking for more ways to include it on your weekly menu, here's a method that even picky eaters will enjoy. The fish cooks up moist and delicious with a coating of garlic, mustard, and herbs. You can swap in other tender herbs—such as dill and chives—depending on what's available and the flavors your family prefers.

SERVES: 4   PREP TIME: 10 minutes   PRESSURE TIME: 2 minutes   RELEASE METHOD: Manual

PREP INGREDIENTS

2   cloves garlic, minced

2   tablespoons olive oil

1   tablespoon Dijon mustard

2   tablespoons chopped parsley

1   teaspoon chopped tarragon
     Salt and black pepper to taste

4   (5- to 6-ounce) fresh salmon fillets, preferably wild-caught

SERVING DAY INGREDIENTS

1   cup water

PREP DIRECTIONS

In a small bowl, mix together the garlic, olive oil, mustard, parsley, and tarragon. Season to taste with salt and pepper. Spread the mixture evenly over the fillets. Place each fillet on a parchment paper–lined sheet of aluminum foil. Wrap each piece individually and place in a 1-gallon resealable freezer bag. Squeeze out the air, seal, label, and freeze.

SERVING DAY DIRECTIONS

Add the water and the trivet to the bottom of the multi-cooker. Place a piece of foil on top of the trivet to catch any drippings. Unwrap the fish and place the fillets on top of the trivet in a single layer (as flat as possible). Cook on low pressure for 2 minutes.

Manually release the pressure. Check for doneness.

INDEX